COUNTDOWN TO
TERROR

COUNTDOWN TO
TERROR

**THE TOP-SECRET INFORMATION THAT COULD
PREVENT THE NEXT TERRORIST ATTACK ON AMERICA...
AND HOW THE CIA HAS IGNORED IT**

CONGRESSMAN

CURT WELDON

Since 1947
**REGNERY
PUBLISHING, INC.**
An Eagle Publishing Company • Washington, DC

Cataloging-in-Publication Data on file
with the Library of Congress

Published in the United States by
Regnery Publishing, Inc.
One Massachusetts Avenue, NW
Washington, DC 20001
www.regnery.com

Distributed to the trade by
National Book Network
Lanham, MD 20706

Manufactured in the United States of America

10 9 8 7 6 5 4 3 2 1

Books are available in quantity for promotional or premium use.
Write to Director of Special Sales, Regnery Publishing, Inc., One
Massachusetts Avenue NW, Washington, DC 20001, for infor-
mation on discounts and terms or call (202) 216-0600.

DEDICATION

To AMERICA'S HEROES in fire departments, emergency rescue services, and the police—our domestic defenders; to our military personnel—our international defenders; to the unsung heroes in the intelligence community—the whistleblowers, dissidents, reformers, and free thinkers; and to America's families—in the hope that they will live in a better, safer world—this book is dedicated.

CONTENTS

ACKNOWLEDGMENTS

To MY WIFE, MY FAMILY, and to all who made this book possible, including Peter Pry, my longtime colleague, friend, and veteran of the CIA, who was invaluable in helping me prepare this manuscript, and to my colleagues and traveling partners Solomon Ortiz, Sylvester Reyes, Roscoe Bartlett, Doug Roach, Russ Caso, Jim Woolsey, Jack Caravelli, and all of those who have believed and encouraged the continuation of the fight for the defense of our nation and our ideals.

1

What You Need to Know

THIS BOOK IS AN ACT OF DESPERATION. I bring it before you, the reader, because I could not get our intelligence community to act on it, though my source has proven his credibility, and though the information he provides predicts a major terrorist attack against the United States.

If the intelligence divulged in this book had been collected by the intelligence community, it would be classified at the highest security level, above TOP SECRET, and would never be seen by the public. I can share this information with you only because it was collected by me, not by the intelligence community. Never before has such "real time," war-related intelligence, from an impeccable clandestine source, been publicly disclosed.

Like all Americans, September 11 is forever seared into my memory. Flames of orange and black exploded from the World Trade Center buildings as airliners struck them like spears. Strangers who hurled themselves into the air and plunged to their deaths to escape the agony of the flames were suddenly as dear to us as brothers and sisters.

Moments earlier, I was speaking at a congressional press conference on national security. My good friends and Democratic colleagues

1

Congressmen Solomon Ortiz and Silvestre Reyes were there. We stood in the Capitol building transfixed by the tragedy unfolding irresistibly before us on the television screen. Now our differences were forgotten, as all of us stood united in horror, pity, anger, and terrible resolve. When the towers crumbled into dust, the shock among us was palpable, as if every person in that crowd was struck a blow. At that moment, I remembered J. Robert Oppenheimer describing what he thought when he witnessed the explosion of the first atomic bomb. It was a line from the Hindu *Bhagavada-Gita*, "I am become death: the destroyer of worlds."

On that terrible day in September, little did I know that I too would soon find myself on the front line in the war on terror, enmeshed in an international intrigue of spies and killers. I was to learn of plots to assassinate world figures—including a former U.S. president—and of a plot to kill hundreds of thousands of Americans by radiation poisoning. I would discover a still more audacious plot, now unfolding, to inflict a terrorist attack on the United States of such catastrophic dimensions that the code name of the attack evokes Shiite Islam's prophet of doom, the twelfth imam, Imam al Mahdi, "*Ya Mahdi, Ad Rekni!*" ("Mahdi save us!"). The twelfth imam miraculously vanished some eleven centuries ago. He is expected to return and fulfill the long-awaited Islamic apocalypse, one that will reward the faithful and, with catastrophic violence, purge all infidels from the face of the Earth.

Fantastic as it might seem, our intelligence community is failing to protect us from this attack, a failure greater than that surrounding September 11. The Central Intelligence Agency (CIA), the Defense Intelligence Agency (DIA), the National Security Agency (NSA)—indeed all of the agencies of the intelligence community—are failing to do what is necessary to prevent the twelfth imam operation.

I am vice chairman of the House Armed Service Committee in Congress and knew before September 11 that our intelligence services were in dire straits. For eight years, the Clinton administration slashed deeply the defense and intelligence budgets, cutting funding for the intelligence community by more then 30 percent. It also pressured the intelligence community to produce "politically correct" intelligence that would serve the needs of administration policy.

This was only the latest blow to the intelligence community. It suffered for decades, and continues to suffer, from serious problems, including an overreliance on technical rather than human intelligence, and a tendency towards politically correct "group think." The result has been a string of intelligence failures.

The Bush administration is working hard to fix our intelligence community. But the fact is that all the efforts of the administration, and Congress, to repair our intelligence posture have failed—at least so far. This was made manifest to me by the stubborn refusal of the intelligence community to do its job and to follow up on the intelligence we have on the 12th Imam plot. It is a refusal that amounts to a dereliction of duty.

I   I   I   I   I   I   I   I   I

As a senior member of Congress responsible for overseeing our nation's defense, I have many people coming to me claiming to know secrets vital to U.S. national security. I do not ignore any of them. All of these people are scrutinized, either by myself, my staff, or by the appropriate federal agencies, which check their *bona fides* to see if they are credible and have anything valuable to offer.

The vast majority of these meetings with potential intelligence sources prove fruitless. In one case, I met a member of the Mafia who claimed to have a scheme that he thought would help the United States capture major terrorists. I turned his case over to the Federal Bureau of Investigation (FBI), who found that he was trying to exploit the war on terrorism in order to work a criminal scam. So I have a healthy skepticism about potential sources.

So it was with low expectations—but enough that I thought I should follow up—that I traveled to Paris in April 2003 to meet a man named "Ali." Ali is the pseudonym for an individual whose information forms the heart of this book, information that he has collected from sources deep within the high command of the terrorist movement. Ali's real name and details cannot be disclosed. I learned of him through unusual channels. On March 7, 2003, at 4:14 p.m., a former Democratic member of Congress and my good friend Ron Klink called and asked to meet with me. His message was that he wished to convey sensitive and urgent information, which he had received from a former CIA operative regarding the location of bin Laden, in addition to other data regarding Iran, derived from a well-connected source. I met with Ron and he outlined the opportunity that we had to obtain more information from this source, which was vital to America's security.

The source was Ali. My contacts with him were at first by telephone. Subsequently, Ali sent faxes to my home on a regular basis from different hotels in Paris, where he lives in exile. Eventually, as the information became more detailed and critical, I decided on a face-to-face meeting. Accompanying me was Dr. Peter Vincent Pry, a trusted adviser and former CIA intelligence officer for ten years.

Ali's background and connections were very impressive and appeared to support his credibility. This much can be told safely, without risking anyone's life: Ali was a former high-ranking member in the government of the shah of Iran. Since the fall of the shah over two decades ago, Ali has been associated with the movement seeking to overthrow the revolutionary government of Iran and its theocratic mullahs. Ali is a close and trusted associate of Manucher Gorbanifar, a controversial figure who played a key role working for the United States during the Iran–Contra affair, and who has been blamed, perhaps wrongly, by the CIA for the failure of the Iran–Contra operation. Although Ali knows Gorbanifar, it is clear that he is independent of him.

Subsequent meetings and encounters with Ali have not shaken my belief in his credibility. Ali himself is knowledgeable and erudite. His personal circumstances, which I am not at liberty to divulge, make it highly unlikely that he would be acting for selfish or illegal reasons. Indeed, Ali's personal circumstances make it likely that he is exactly what he appears to be: a true patriot who wishes to see an Iran that is democratic, civilized, and an adversary of global terrorism.

Although Ali's credentials were impressive, Dr. Pry and I emerged from our first meeting nearly convinced that he was a fraud. Ali made fantastic claims about the advanced status of Iran's nuclear weapons program, Iranian cooperation with North Korea on nuclear weapons, terrorist plans for attacks in Europe and the United States, Iranian plans to destabilize the situation in Iraq by supporting terrorism and clandestine operations there, and other extraordinary claims. Ali's allegations were sharply at variance with unclassified estimates of the U.S. intelligence community. Ali's views also disagreed with the "common wisdom" of the defense, academic, and press communities. Basically, if Ali was right, then everyone else was wrong.

For example, Ali told us that Iran's atomic bomb program was very advanced and near completion, so near that they might soon perform a nuclear test. Yet at the time Ali spoke to us, unclassified intelligence community estimates and "common wisdom" held that Iran's atomic program was still in its infancy. Ali told us that Iran was seeking cooperation with North Korea on its nuclear weapons program. He said Iran even attempted to buy an atomic bomb from North Korea. No one in the West—or the East—was reporting such alarming developments. Ali said that Iran was the primary supporter of insurgents in Iraq, while everyone else was saying that Syria was the culprit. Ali said that Osama bin Laden was hiding in Iran, an honored guest. But the U.S. military was then and still is searching for bin Laden in Afghanistan and Pakistan. Later, Ali told us that there was a terrorist plot to hijack a Canadian airliner and fly it into a nuclear reactor in the United States. Such an attack could kill hundreds of thousands of Americans through radiation poisoning. All of this sounded so incredible that Dr. Pry and I left that first meeting with Ali just shaking our heads.

Yet as the weeks and months passed, Ali's predictions and his version of events either came true or were independently verified, often becoming the stuff of newspaper headlines. Indeed, the day after our first meeting with Ali, some unconfirmed press reports alleged that North Korea had announced that it reserved the right to sell nuclear weapons to other states. This was consistent with Ali's claim that Iran was seeking to purchase an atomic bomb from North Korea. Later, a North Korean defector disclosed that Iranian delegations had in fact gone to North Korea seeking cooperation on their nuclear weapons programs and to buy an atomic bomb. A year and a half later, an unclassified CIA report confirmed that North Korea threatened secretly to sell nuclear weapons ("in late April 2003") exactly when Ali had warned us of this threat. The story made headlines in the *Washington Times* (November 27, 2004).

Also in November 2004, *U.S. News and World Report* ran a cover story, allegedly based on classified intelligence reports, proving that Iran was the primary engine driving the insurgency in Iraq, just as Ali had told us in Paris. Ali's information about the Iranian connection to Iraq predated *by months* the earliest classified intelligence cited by *U.S. News and World Report*. And again in November 2004, CIA analysts publicly observed that the clerical robes worn by Osama bin Laden in a video message suggested that he might be hiding among a religious order located in Iran. Perhaps most remarkably, in August 2003, a terrorist cell was arrested in Canada, apparently plotting to fly a hijacked airliner into a nuclear reactor in the United States, again as Ali had warned.

Many other predictions of Ali turned out to be true. As time passed and Ali's many allegations were uncanny in their accuracy, he built for me an impressive track record. As the reader will find in the documents that follow, the course of world events have established incontrovertibly that Ali is a highly credible source of reliable intelligence on Iranian and other terrorist activities.

ı   ı   ı   ı   ı   ı   ı   ı   ı   ı

Before events proved Ali to be an excellent resource in the war on terrorism, I provided all of his information to the intelligence community, and asked them to evaluate him. Ali's impressive background and connections alone warranted further investigation of his extraordinary claims. We just could not risk another major intelligence failure that might lead to a repeat of September 11, perhaps on a far more destructive scale.

Because of the nature of Ali's claims, I believed it important that I meet personally with George Tenet, then director of the CIA. I asked Tenet to have the CIA meet with Ali, evaluate him, and work with him if the agency judged he might be useful. Because of Ali's background and connections, I assumed the CIA would employ him. The CIA routinely places people on its payroll whose credentials are far less impressive than Ali's.

Tenet appeared interested, even enthusiastic, about evaluating Ali and establishing a working relationship with him. He agreed to send his top spy, Stephen Kappes, the deputy director of operations, along with me to Paris for another debriefing of Ali. It was at this point that I entered the "wilderness of mirrors." On the day of our scheduled second meeting with Ali in Paris, Kappes bowed out, claiming that "other commitments" compelled him to cancel. Given the high stakes in the war on terrorism, and the well-known fact that the CIA is desperately deficient in human intelligence sources—and that the meeting had been blessed by Kappes's superior, Tenet—I found it hard to imagine what "other commitments" could have possibly been more compelling. Later, the CIA claimed to have met with Ali independently. But I discovered this to be untrue. The CIA admitted this, with no explanation as to why they would lie to me about the meeting.

Incredibly, I learned that the CIA had apparently asked French intelligence to silence Ali. Ali had had no contact with the French Ministry of Interior, France's equivalent of the FBI, for many years. Yet shortly after the CIA discovered Ali was talking to me, an agent from the French Ministry of Interior requested a meeting with Ali to discuss what he knew about terrorism. Although the French agent did not overtly threaten Ali, Ali nonetheless regarded the meeting as ominous, given its close coincidence with the time he was supposed to meet with the CIA. The purpose of the French Ministry of Interior appears to have been to intimidate Ali.

Weeks later, the CIA finally met with Ali. But the agency's purpose was to chastise him and threaten him for talking to a member of Congress. Point blank, Ali was warned to shut his mouth and stop talking to Curt Weldon.

Meanwhile, I tried to work with Stephen Kappes. I encouraged Kappes to investigate Ali's credentials and offered to set up another meeting. Finally, Kappes threatened me too. He warned me to stop working with Ali. He said it was a violation of U.S. law for an American citizen to meet with a foreign agent. I know the law. His claim was preposterous and I told him so. Kappes then warned me that it might be dangerous for my personal safety to associate with someone like Ali.

Fortunately, Kappes has now resigned from the CIA. He resigned after unsuccessfully challenging the leadership of the new CIA director, Porter Goss. Kappes was the ringleader of an internal CIA rebellion. He was one of many in the CIA resistant to needed reforms.

Even with Kappes gone, the CIA has yet to establish a working relationship with Ali. I wanted the CIA to do its job and not leave me to do the work of an intelligence agent. But, unlike the CIA, I could not simply walk away from the situation and forget the dire warnings coming from Ali. The CIA never offered me a good reason why Ali should be ignored, and because the agency would not do its job, I was obligated to do it. For nearly two years, I collected—and continue to collect—intelligence from him, forwarding it to the intelligence community and other relevant authorities.

The Secret Service, to its credit, did take seriously Ali's warning of a terrorist plot to assassinate the president's father, former president George H. W. Bush. The Secret Service met with Ali, but Ali's other intelligence, on broader national security threats, is not actionable by the Secret Service. The terrorist threat to President Bush's father, as you shall read later, remains active, but the Secret Service is alert to it, because they took seriously the intelligence I provided to them.

It is even more astounding that the intelligence community continues to ignore Ali after he predicted a major terrorist attack on the United States, which could have killed hundreds of thousands of Americans. This attack would have far exceeded September 11 in the scale of destruction and loss of human life. As I mentioned earlier, Ali warned that terrorists were plotting to hijack an airliner in Canada so they could fly it into a nuclear reactor in the United States. In August 2003, a terrorist cell composed of Muslim males eighteen to thirty-three years old, all from Pakistan, with the exception of one Indian, was arrested in Toronto, apparently planning to do exactly this. The terrorists had been undergoing pilot training in Canada. They were practicing flying over a Canadian nuclear reactor and making visits on the ground to the reactor, seemingly to familiarize themselves with a similar target in the United States.

It turned out that the terrorists were apparently planning to attack the Seabrook Nuclear Reactor, located in a populous region just forty miles from Boston. The terrorists' actions indicated that once again an airplane was to be used as a missile, this time crashing into a nuclear reactor. The resulting explosion and fire would have caused a poisonous radioactive cloud covering thousands of square miles, as happened after the accident at Chernobyl in the Soviet Union almost two decades ago. We know from the Chernobyl experience that the plume from a burning nuclear reactor is extremely deadly. It can create elevated and dangerous levels of radiation over vast areas, covering perhaps several states. Had the terrorists succeeded in their apparent attack on the Seabrook site, they must have hoped the plume would cover Boston and the populous areas of the northeast United States, killing hundreds of thousands of Americans by radiation poisoning.

I believe Ali thwarted the impending attack on a U.S. nuclear reactor. We provided the intelligence community with Ali's warning, including details about the plot, months before the arrests occurred. It seems an impossible coincidence that Ali anticipated this threat and then law enforcement agencies just happened to find the perpetrators, and stopped the attack from happening, as if by accident. This success alone should have established Ali's credibility and reliability within the intelligence community. Absurdly, the CIA claimed that the information he was giving to me probably came from open press sources, available to anyone. But a little research soon proved this to be false.

To rebut the CIA's assertion that Ali's information was coming from open press sources, I turned to the Congressional Research Service (CRS). The CRS, through the Foreign Broadcast Information Service and other means, can keep track of all print, radio, and television press reports worldwide. Without telling the CRS the full details of the Ali situation, both for security reasons and to preserve their objectivity, we asked their researchers to find the earliest press reports on a number of international developments that had been predicted by Ali. The idea was to find if any of these important events appeared in the press first, as the CIA claimed, or if Ali had made the prediction before the development was reported in the press. In not a single case did the CRS find any press, television, or radio reports, anywhere in the world, which Ali could have relied on to fake his predictions. Ali's warnings were consistently days, weeks, or months in advance of their first appearance in the press. The bottom line from the CRS was that Ali's record of forecasting was consistent with his claim that he had

WHAT YOU NEED TO KNOW

access to sensitive, inside information derived from high-ranking sources within the government of Iran.

Next, I turned to my friend Porter Goss, then chairman of the House Permanent Select Committee on Intelligence (HPSCI). I explained the Ali situation to Porter. I sent Porter and Pat Roberts, chairman of the Senate Select Committee on Intelligence (SSCI), all of the Ali materials and the sad history of the CIA's strange behavior, warning that this constituted a dangerous "intelligence failure in the process of happening."

For once, this pushed the CIA in a constructive direction. Agents again met with Ali and promised to work with him. But it was all for show. As soon as the attention of the HPSCI and SSCI turned to other matters, the CIA abandoned Ali and did not follow through on their promise to work with him. It is obvious that the CIA's temporary good behavior was only a pretense to deceive the congressional oversight committees. The DIA and the NSA also chose to ignore Ali.

Why the intelligence community stubbornly refuses to work with Ali remains a mystery. I have several theories, but none is adequate alone to account for such a gross dereliction of duty.

Incompetence. It would not be the first time that the intelligence community has failed to appreciate the importance of a source. During the Cold War, the CIA turned down the Soviet defector Vasili Mitrokhin, who defected instead to the British. As a KGB (Soviet Committee of State Security or "secret police") archivist, Mitrokhin turned out to be one of the most important sources on KGB operations in history. The CIA's failure to recruit Mitrokhin was a huge blunder. Unfortunately, the Mitrokhin fiasco is not an isolated case.

Obsolete Approach. During the Cold War, the CIA and other U.S. intelligence agencies became accustomed to virtually "owning" their sources. People who were willing to serve as spies within the Soviet system usually did so for ideological reasons, not for money. These idealists were often willing to comply with any demand that the CIA would make of them, even at the risk of their lives. One of the CIA's chief complaints against Ali is that he is not willing to divulge the identity of his sources to them. Ali argues that this is unacceptable, as it would make him completely subservient to the CIA. Nor does he trust the CIA to protect his sources. In the war on terrorism, the CIA cannot expect to find many ideological idealists who are willing to let the CIA "own" them, and completely subordinate their interests to those of the CIA. The CIA's approach is obsolete.

Institutional Memory. Ali's friendship with Manucher Gorbanifar may account for the CIA's refusal to work with him. The CIA blames Gorbanifar for the failure of its Iran–Contra operation, and has come to regard him as an enemy. Gorbanifar claims that the CIA made him the scapegoat for the humiliating Iran–Contra affair, and has come to believe its own propaganda, from nearly two decades ago.

Fear. The intelligence community might not want to work with Ali precisely because he is an excellent source of startling intelligence on terrorist activities and Iran's programs for weapons of mass destruction (WMD), and because he is associated with the Iranian counter-revolutionary movement. The CIA, DIA, and NSA know that the U.S. military is stretched thin prosecuting the war against terrorism in Iraq and Afghanistan. There is a looming crisis with North Korea, which may soon pose another challenge to the U.S. military. Simply put, the United States at this moment cannot afford to become entangled in war against Iran. The intelligence community may fear that this is precisely what could happen by working with Ali.

Ali's intelligence on Iran's illegal atomic bomb program, on Iran's support for terrorist operations against U.S. troops in Iraq, and on Iran's support of international terrorism worldwide is sufficiently alarming to justify a military response from the United States. Indeed, the apparent terrorist operation to attack a U.S. nuclear reactor and destroy Boston was, again according to Ali, directed from Tehran. This alone is a reason for a military response, a legitimate *casus belli*.

Moreover, the intelligence community probably does not want to become entangled with an Iranian counter-revolutionary movement that it cannot control. Were Iranian freedom fighters to rise up against the oppressive government of Iran and fail, would the U.S. government turn its back on them, if it could be shown they had received even tacit support from the United States? Almost certainly not, since President George W. Bush well remembers the slaughter of the Shiite and Kurdish freedom fighters in Iraq during the first Gulf War. They were encouraged to rise up by the U.S. government, then abandoned. President Bush would not allow another stain on American honor by abandoning U.S.-supported freedom fighters in Iran. The intelligence community may be avoiding Ali like the plague, despite his excellent intelligence, because they want to avoid, at all costs, drawing the United States into a war with Iran.

But the stakes in the war on terrorism are too high to turn down an intelligence source like Ali, whether out of incompetence, old habits, or some other misguided Machiavellian reason.

The simple truth is that we cannot afford to ignore the kind of intelligence that Ali has to offer. Ali's sources in the Iranian counter-revolutionary movement have penetrated two vital targets:

- The Committee of Nine. Headed by Ayatollah Khameni, this elite committee is a secret organization that plans international terrorist operations, including operations involving al Qaeda, Islamic Jihad, Hezbollah, Ansar al Islam, and other major terrorist organizations. Iran is the world's leading sponsor of international terrorism through the Committee of Nine.

- WMD Programs. Iran's programs for nuclear, biological, and chemical weapons and missiles are of vital interest to the United States. The Committee of Nine may make WMD available to international terrorists.

Ali's intelligence represents an opportunity that is rare in history. He is equivalent to the Soviet spy "Werther," who, during World War II, penetrated the German General Staff and gave to Moscow secret war plans that proved decisive in defeating Hitler's "Operation Citadel" in 1943. This espionage triumph helped seal the fate of Nazi Germany and was important in the Allied victory during World War II. Ali is also comparable to Colonel Oleg Penkovsky, "The Spy Who Saved the World" (as his biography is titled), who provided vital information to the United States on the Soviet nuclear weapons program. Ali offers to the United States the same kind of decisive, war-winning intelligence in the struggle against terrorism.

I believe Ali has already helped save hundreds of thousands of American lives. The reader should know that Ali's information provided so far is only a sample of what he is capable of collecting. The amazing intelligence given to the United States by Ali over the past two years has been begged and purchased out of his own pocket. It has been provided by his sources in Iran on the understanding that much more money would be forthcoming, the kind of money that could be raised, for example, by the CIA. The intelligence contained in the pages of this book was intended to establish the *bona fides* of Ali's sources to the satisfaction of the U.S. intelligence community. This intelligence merely hints at the much richer intelligence that is available, for the right price. Dare we remain ignorant, can we survive, without the early warning and operational details available through Ali on these threats to the United States?

- The 12th Imam Operation—when, where, and what is this act of catastrophic terrorism planned against the United States?

- Weapons of Mass Destruction—how near is Iran to the atomic bomb, to biological and chemical weapons, and will its leaders give them to terrorists?

- Iraq—what operations are planned against U.S. troops in Iraq and to replace a democratic Iraq with an Islamic state?

- International Terrorism—what terror operations are planned against U.S. allies in Europe and Asia?

- Assassinations—who is targeted and what are the operational details?

Congressmen with the highest security clearances entrusted to work on defense issues are not supposed to "go public" with sensitive intelligence. However, September 11 showed that terrorists have ample knowledge of our intelligence community's incompetence. They will not be helped or encouraged by my revelations. If for one moment I thought otherwise, this book would have never appeared. The only people being kept in the dark are the American people. Washington's top defense and intelligence bureaucrats will no doubt strongly condemn me for this book. But the Founding Fathers conceived a last resort: To go outside of government, directly to the American people.

For two years now, I have tried to work with the intelligence community. I even appealed to the House and Senate intelligence oversight committees. All the normal processes for achieving a "meeting of the minds" with the intelligence community have been exhausted. I find myself with no alternative but to turn to you, the American people. When there is a problem in our system so deep that Washington alone cannot fix it, only pressure from the people can force Washington to act, and to act quickly.

You see, the intelligence community burned me once before. I will never forgive myself for not pushing harder to establish a capability, which could have given our nation and our president a threat assessment that 9/11 was in the planning stages and about to occur.

In the spring of 1999, I led eleven members of Congress in a bipartisan delegation to Vienna, two weeks after the bombing of Belgrade started. I led this delegation, which was initiated at the request of every major Russian political party and with the full support of the Clinton administration's State Department, to attempt to find a framework to end the

Kosovo war and remove Slobodan Milosevic from power. Before leaving for Vienna, I personally contacted George Tenet and requested a profile of a Serb who the Russians told me they were bringing to Vienna, allegedly because of his access to Milosevic and his supporters. I wanted to make sure that this individual was not a part of the Milosevic regime. Tenet followed up my request within a day and told me the CIA had little information on the Serb but that they were certain that he was not a part of the Milosovic regime; not much else was available that could give me insight into this individual, whom the Russians were convinced could help end the war.

At the time, as chairman of the Defense Research Subcommittee of the House Armed Services Committee, I had been aggressively pushing and "plussing-up" funding for the Army's Information Dominance Center (LIWA—Land Information Warfare Assistance Center) at Fort Belvoir. I had been made aware of the tremendous and amazing capability created by massive data mining, data fusion, and data collaboration of disparate intelligence systems and the resultant technical ability to do profiling of emerging transnational threats and individuals.

I telephoned my Army friends "off the record" and asked them for an "unofficial" profile of the Serb, which the CIA could not give me. The LIWA, within a matter of hours, gave me ten pages (even though it was unvetted) of information about the man who would be traveling to Vienna with the Russians.

On returning to the United States, after having successfully developed a two-page framework to end the Kosovo war on our terms, with full Russian support in addition to Milosovic's intent to embrace publicly the framework and to release two well-publicized American POWs to my delegation, I was immediately contacted separately by the CIA and the FBI. They requested that I meet with their agents as soon as possible for the purpose of debriefing them on what I knew about the Serb and his family.

Even though the CIA had pressed me to meet over the weekend, I convinced the agency to be debriefed jointly with the FBI on Monday in my office. At 3:00 p.m., on Monday, May 24, 1999, I hosted four agents for the purpose of providing information on the Serbian family with whom my delegation had met. These agents had been tasked to brief the State Department's ambassador negotiating the final terms of the Kosovo peace settlement on the Serbs.

After briefing the four agents, I asked them where they thought I had acquired my information on the Serb and his family. The agents said that I probably got my information from the Russians or perhaps from the Serb himself. "No," I said, "I got all of the information that I just passed to you from the Army's Information Dominance Center." With that, the agents collectively asked me what the Army's Information Dominance Center was! (I learned this past year from the State Department that on the same date basic information that I had provided was placed in the official visa files of the Serbian family.)

It was then that I knew that our intelligence capability regarding emerging transnational threats was woefully inadequate, because our intelligence community was not working as a team. I had a responsibility to act and change this situation. Starting in May 1999, I developed, with the assistance of friends within the intelligence and LIWA establishments, a nine-page brief to create the National Operations and Analysis Hub (NOAH), which would force the disparate agencies of the intelligence community to work together.

The deputy secretary of defense at the time, John Hamre, became very interested in the NOAH concept, and, at my suggestion, went down to the LIWA for a personal briefing. He actually tasked the LIWA staff to run an assessment for him of their capabilities.

As I began to press the administration for development of NOAH, Hamre suggested that he would support such a capability with Department of Defense (DOD) funds and allow the center to be housed wherever the White House and president wanted, but that I would first have to convince the CIA and FBI, over which he had no control, to agree to such a concept.

At Hamre's suggestion, on November 4, 1999, I arranged a meeting in my Washington office with Hamre and his counterparts at the FBI and the CIA. I provided the brief to all three officials personally. The brief was entitled "National Operations and Analysis Hub: Policy Makers Tool for Acting Against Emerging Transnational Threats and Dangers to U.S. National Security," and described an overarching plan to fuse intelligence data from all thirty-three classified systems of the federal intelligence bureaucracy. It also mandated use of "open source" data, which was not being used by the CIA in their threat assessments.

When I finished the briefing, the agents from the FBI and CIA said, "Congressman, we really don't need this capability." Frustrated, but undaunted, I continued to hold classified and open hearings on this intelligence need. I gave numerous speeches to intelligence gatherings. I even inserted language in three successive defense authorization bills requiring continuing DOD pursuit of intelligence system collaboration. Because the defense authorization bills have no jurisdiction over the CIA or FBI, I could not mandate their participation or cooperation.

Then 9/11 happened and the need for the capability to share intelligence reached a crisis point. I wanted our government to act quickly. On September 25, 2001, just two weeks after 9/11, I met in the White House with Stephen Hadley, the deputy national security adviser to the president. I presented him with a 2' × 3' chart I had been given in the aftermath of 9/11. The chart was developed in 1999, as part of a Defense Department initiative dubbed "Able Danger." It diagrammed the affiliations of al Qaeda and showed Mohammed Atta and the infamous Brooklyn Cell. Hadley's response was, "I have to show this to the big man." Information such as this, which was apparently available but not widely distributed to key U.S. officials, made NOAH even more of a priority.

Two years before 9/11, I gave our intelligence community a plan, a system, and a challenge to end the "stovepipes" created by thirty-three classified systems operated by some sixteen different federal agencies and jurisdictions. Intelligence community officials did not listen. Not only did the intelligence community during the Clinton administration not pursue this capability, it was not until the State of the Union speech by President Bush in January 2003 that the president himself announced his intention to create an entity identical to NOAH, the Terrorist Threat Integration Center (TTIC). The TTIC began its work in May 2003, four years after I proposed my plan.

It will forever be emblazoned in my mind that I should have pushed harder and not allowed bureaucrats in the intelligence community to brush aside so cavalierly such a crucial and vital initiative that could have given us insights into what was being planned against our nation. While we will never know whether or not NOAH could have prevented 9/11, its capability would have certainly afforded us a better understanding of what was about to occur.

So, I have no choice but to write this book. Ali has given me information that has been corroborated completely. The intelligence community has not refuted any of Ali's claims. They have only repeatedly asked for his "sources," which he would obviously not provide.

As my book outlines, Ali claims to know how to get the full details of the next planned (and already named) attack against the Unites States, as well as the location of bin Laden. I have every obligation, personally and professionally, to pursue that information to its completion and to push once again against the bureaucracy of American intelligence.

As a former fire chief, founder and chairman emeritus of the Congressional Fire/EMS Institute and Caucus and champion for the 1.2 million first responders who grieved the loss of 343 brother firefighters on 9/11, including my good friend Chief Ray Downey, I will never let America pass up another opportunity to understand emerging threats to our security, whether from North Korea, Iran, or terrorist individuals and groups. I invite you to join me in this effort.

My hope is that this book will make you angry, angry enough to act, and save American lives. If it is successful, this book will keep alive the demand of the American people following the 9/11 attacks to reform

U.S. intelligence. What has been accomplished so far, and what will be accomplished by prospective reforms, is not nearly enough. We need to keep the reform process going. Right now, even the most ambitious reforms proposed do little more than move the chairs around the deck of the Titanic. Unless more is done, much more, we may well lose the war on terrorism.

What you are about to read are memos written over the last two years from Ali to me. The memos are divided chronologically, into monthly chapters. Each chapter is preceded by a brief précis, or introduction, that provides historical context and highlights the memos and their significance.

You should be warned that English is Ali's fourth language, so his grammar and syntax can be slightly awkward. But I thought it important for you see the raw intelligence as I received it. You can judge for yourself whether the intelligence being offered by Ali is important, whether the intelligence community is right to ignore him, and whether I have acted rightly in appealing to you, the American people.

2

ALI REPORTS

22–25 April 2003

"To face up to the United States, a global comprehensive
and aggressive approach has been worked out."

—*Committee of Nine*

APRIL 2003 SAW THE LIGHTNING VICTORY of United States and coalition forces over Saddam Hussein. The Iraqi dictator's giant statue in
central Baghdad is toppled by the U.S. Marines, to the approval of
cheering crowds. Terrorist Abu Abbas, responsible for the 1985 attack
on Italian cruise ship *Achille Lauro*, is captured. U.S. Special Forces
capture also Barzan Ibrahim al Tikrit, Saddam's half-brother and intelligence chief on the United States' "most wanted" list. Tariq Aziz, Iraqi
deputy prime minister and the international face of Saddam Hussein's
government, surrenders. American and allied forces are welcomed by
most of the Iraqi people as liberators.

In April 2003, the terrorist campaign against U.S. and allied forces and
against the Iraqi people has not yet begun and there is as yet no inkling
of a looming nuclear crisis over Iran's development of an atomic
bomb. In the *New York Times*, one of the big stories on Iran is that
actress Gowhar Kheirandish gets a suspended sentence of seventy-four
lashes after apologizing for kissing director Ali Zamani.

At my first meeting with Ali, on April 25, 2003, he provided me with his first report, dated April 22, 2003. Also in this chapter is my report on what Ali told me at our April 25 meeting.

I provided both reports to the intelligence community immediately. Among the many startling allegations in the reports, Ali warned:

- Iran is sponsoring a terrorist plot to assassinate President Bush's father, George H. W. Bush.

- Osama bin Laden is hiding in Iran, in a specific location identified by Ali.

- Iran has a crash program to build an atomic bomb that is more advanced than generally credited in the West.

- Iran is seeking nuclear cooperation, and trying to purchase an A-bomb, from North Korea.

- Iranian-sponsored terrorists and Iranian agents of the Revolutionary Guard are building a terror network in Iraq to attack U.S. and allied forces and to kill Iraqi democracy in the cradle.

- Iran's Committee of Nine supports and manages international terrorist operations, working with al Qaeda, Hezbollah, Islamic Jihad, Ansar al Islam, and other major terrorist groups. Ali's report provides actual minutes from a meeting of the Committee of Nine.

Ali's April 22 report, in addition to warning about the threat from Tehran, is also basically a blueprint for mounting a counter-revolution in Iran. It even identifies many of the leaders of the counter-revolutionary movement. These names have been deleted here.

The proximity of an Iranian atomic bomb can be inferred from Ali's information that Iran hoped to conduct its first nuclear test in September 2003. In a later report, the atomic test is postponed because the schedule is too ambitious, and from fear that a nuclear test might provoke a war with the United States.

Ali's allegation that Yasser Arafat would be assassinated in the near future was long regarded by us as a rare example of bad information from him. Yasser Arafat died in November 2004 of mysterious causes. Many claim that Arafat was poisoned, as is suggested by his symptoms. Did the Committee of Nine kill Arafat, as Ali said they would, after all?

04/22/03 REPORT

As mentioned in our previous report, on the order of Khameni, the military and security forces having analyzed their strategy, policies, and tactics—in light of the unexpected collapse of Iraq—have submitted their reports to Khameni.

The Committee of Nine was called into session on 4/18/2003 to study the conclusions of the reports and receive the orders of the Leader.

Due to the presence of several members of the military and the security forces, the number of participants temporarily increased from 9 to 15. Rafsandjani was absent from this meeting. The meeting lasted 7 hours and 15 reports were discussed.

Since Mollah Hashemi (Mirhajazi) already received the written reports of the military and security forces, and heard the oral briefings, he started the discussions with this summary:

"To face up to the U.S., a global-comprehensive and aggressive approach has been worked out."

- "All forces would have to increase their readiness for defense purposes."

- "Antiaircraft defenses would be strengthened, mainly to more efficiently defend important centers."

- "The Air Force would play a complementary role."

- "Generally speaking, the Armed Forces would concentrate their fighting power around and within big cities. For this purpose, tunnels would be built within the towns."

- "The military forces of the Army, Pasdaran, Basij are well-equipped: Missiles purchased in China, 1500 Kornet AT missiles from Russia, new AT-ARPG11s, provide us with the necessary fire power to destroy the American aggressor. Even the TOWS manufactured in Iran, can destroy the best American tanks."

- "A squadron of 45 suicide aircraft with pilots trained for this purpose and prepared for martyrdom, are ready to attack US targets, mainly at sea."

KHAMENI then expressed his satisfaction with the military reports and stated:

"The US shall realize very quickly that we are not like Iraq. Iran shall be the hell for the U.S. The Americans say that Iran is a cancerous tumor in the region. That is correct in the sense that Iran as such, will destroy the entire body of the U.S. We have to assume that the U.S. will attack us during this presidency or in Bush's second term, if re-elected. The Americans believe that they can topple our regime with a people's revolution. We cannot trust a fox. They may say one thing and do the opposite. For this reason, we must be ready for any kind of American move. Concerning any military move, we are prepared. Concerning any popular uprising, we should do whatever is necessary, so that the Americans lose their illusions".

"For this purpose, I have already instructed our security and intelligence formations:"

a. "To suppress all demonstrations"

b. "To prevent any new figure from becoming too popular, we shall use techniques that we employed years ago. We will have people disguised as international reporters along with TV teams to arrange interviews. This is how we will recognize the dissidents."

"There is no room for dissent. I have also informed KHA-TAMI of my decision and I think he will come along. Raf-sandjani also fully supports my decision. In any case, anybody in this meeting who doesn't agree can resign, and even go abroad."

All members present voice their support of KHAMENI.

KHAMENI continued: "We are not only ready for any move by the U.S., but we shall take the initiative because our approach is comprehensive and aggressive. For example, should the foreign office send us a message concerning an inspection of our facilities, everyone should know that no one can issue an ultimatum to us. We shall issue ultimatums to others!! When I say that we shall take the initiative in opposing the U.S., I mean the following:"

- "We have received a report from our General Pasdar Bigdali in Baghdad, informing us that the possibilities of targeting the U.S. in Iraq are unlimited. We have 500 reliable agents in Iraq, among them, 26 Mullahs. *I have given orders that our people start operations against American targets from 'Arbein' (Tuesday, 04/22/03) in the same way we did in Lebanon.*"

- "In this context, I have instructed our Iraqi Coordination Committee that unlimited financial help be provided for action there."

- "We have already discussed the U.S. threat to Syria and informed the Syrian government that they can rely on our support in the event of any U.S. attack. Hezballah is also prepared to act forcefully in such a case."

- "Mohssen Rezai, is coordinating our actions with Emad Moghnie, Aniss Nagash and Nasrollah."

- "Seven (7) members of Al Qaeda in the USA and Canada, who played a logistic role on September 11, have been in contact with us and are prepared to act again. They already have the necessary **chemical and biological** products; but we shall also be supplying them with our products from our sources in Golestan (in Western Iran). Furthermore, we shall notify our fifth column abroad to begin targeting American interests."

End of meeting report.

Additional intelligence information:

- Three (3) high ranking Iraqis are now in Iran. They will be sent to Shiraz.

- A number of high ranking Iraqis have passed through Syria on their way to Yemen and Libya.

- A large number of high ranking, Iraqi families have already arrived in Egypt and Europe.

INFORMATION OF CURRENT IMPORTANCE

1. As of Tuesday, 22 April 2003, agents of Iran will begin to initiate civil disturbances, bombings, assassinations and terrorist activities against the U.S. occupation of Iraq. Teams of terrorists, arms, explosives and equipment are already moving over the border from Iran to Iraq.

2. Agency personnel in Iraq should immediately attempt to locate and recruit former members of the Mujahedin Khalq. This was a foreign legion of Iranians established by Saddam

Hussein in Iraq to destabilize Iran. Given new direction, betters support and leadership, many of the members of this organization could be very useful in our project.

3. The time is now ideal for organizing and assisting various groups in Iran that want to bring about a change in this regime. Without assistance, these groups may fail—setting back any hopes for a non-war regime change for years to come. Since current U.S. human assets in Iran are minimal, we want to directly participate in bringing about a change in regime.

PROGRAM

1. 19 Companies:

In order to preserve security while financing its terror operations outside of Iran and avoiding legislative oversight, the hardliners (HL) have established thirty-two (32) separate companies. We can furnish the names and details of these companies; as well as documentation as to their structure, organization and activities.

2. Osama Bin Laden and Ayman al-Zawahiri:

It has been reported that both of the above subjects have been given sanctuary in Iran. Both were located in five (5) building settlement, a few miles from Ladiz in Baluchistan on the Iranian side of the Pakistan/Iran/Afghanistan border. On 21 March, we heard that both subjects were moved from Ladiz to Kerman and from Kerman to Tehran. Near Tehran, in the northern suburb of Saltanatbad (now called Pasdaran) they were placed in (Sawama safe-house) villas with special, in-ground-secure (formerly SAVAK) telephone lines. Sanctuary was granted on the basis of cooperation in on-going projects.

With proper street maps, we should be able to pinpoint the areas down to specific villa addresses and coordinates.

3. **Committee of Nine:**

After the collapse of the Baath regime in Iraq, which completely surprised Tehran, a "Committee of Nine" was established to formulate Iran's reaction, strategy, and policy to this new development. The committee principals are the Khameni, Rafsandjani, Mohssen Rezai, and the Heads of Sepah, Mullah Hashemi—in charge of coordination of assets from Al Qaeda, Hamas, Hezballah, and Taliban subversive elements in Afghanistan, and a new, unnamed, high-level representative of the Foreign Ministry, who belongs fully to Khamenei, and shares no information with Khatami or his Minister of Foreign Affairs.

The meeting was opened by a report of the new representative of the Ministry of Foreign Affairs. The representative stated, "We should not forget that the 'old fox', George Bush had stated in 1992 before the election that he would get rid of the Mullahs in Tehran, if he were reelected. Today, behind the scenes, this 'old fox' is still in charge." At this stage, Mullah Hashemi intervened and said, "He is a good target and we should try to get rid of him. He is a much easier target than the President since he is less protected."

At that point, the representative of the Ministry of Foreign Affairs stated that, "any contact with US will have a bad effect on the Guardians of the Revolution and the Bassij and weaken their morale and fighting spirit."

Khameni gave full support to the statement and added, "If the U.S. thinks that it can do the same thing that they did in Iraq to us— they are completely wrong. We have studied their strategy and we shall adapt our forces and strategy. Not only do we have all the arms that Iraq did not use, we have even much more. It will be

HELL for the U.S. Furthermore, Khameni continued, "We have our fifth column outside Iran and we shall strike American interest throughout the world and in the United States. And it is interesting to note, that even the British are not even supporting the USA."

The reaction among those present was far from approval. Mullah Hashemi reacting said, "It looks like Rafsandjani has forgotten martyrdom and prefers his existence in this world." One of the Heads of Sepah joined in by saying, "We need only to play around until May" and prevent any improvised inspections of our installations. Then, we will be in a position of power and everybody will have to negotiate with us and we can impose our own will." To this, Rafsandjani retorted, "We still need to discuss everything!" Khameni then made the closing statement, "Remember! No one has the right to have contacts with the United States."

Next Thursday, 24 April 2003, all of the leaders of Iran's military forces will meet and submit their reports to Khameni on the proposed changes of strategy and tactics for facing the U.S.

Notes:

- North Korea is cooperating very closely in the supply of missiles and technology.

- China is keeping some distance

- Russia is supplying RPG-11's with Night Sights and Kornet AT Missiles. May 2003 is a significant date to the Committee of Nine in that this is the month when the Committee members expect the first nuclear weapon will be available for deployment. There are 375 contracted "experts" from Russia, ex-CIS countries, Serbia, and North Korea working in Iran for the production of nuclear weapons. These 375 experts are in addition to the official number of Russian technicians working on

power stations in the south that are already acknowledged by the government of Iran.

4. Terrorist Cooperation:

We will be able to secure information on the lines of commu-
nication, cooperation, and specific joint projects between the
Committee of Nine and Al Qaeda, Hezballah, Hamas, Islamic
Jihad and Hekmatyar (Afghanistan).

5. Other Terrorists:

We can provide detailed information on the following persons,
their locations and their activities: Emade Mognie, Aniss
Nagash, and Morteza Rezai—the Head of Sepah's Intelligence.

6. Pakistan and Afghanistan:

We can provide information on the operations of Sepah in Pakistan and Afghanistan.

7. Access:

We have access to specific persons in authority in Iran that will
cooperate with us to bring about a change in the regime.

IRANIAN ANALYSIS AND STRATEGIES

The current attitude of a number of reform-minded, high-level
religious leaders and theologians: Religion today faces many
critical problems in Iran as a result of the policies of the hardliners. Religion's place in society is now being questioned, as
well as its role in guiding and influencing peoples' thoughts
and behavior. To give religion back its historical, cultural and
moral legitimacy, one of the most important priorities is the

separation of State and Religion. Fortunately the majority of the most important theologians (other than those running the country) are fully aware of this priority, and ready to take the lead in supporting our efforts to bring about a change in regime. We are in continuous contact with all of the like-minded theologians, and have made the necessary arrangements for their cooperation. Below are listed those theologians who are ready to cooperate in this project. They are listed by location.

QOM:

- [NAME DELETED]
- [NAME DELETED]
- [NAME DELETED]
- [NAME DELETED]

TEHRAN:

- [NAME DELETED]
- [NAME DELETED]
- [NAME DELETED]
- [NAME DELETED]

MASHHAD:

- [NAME DELETED]
- [NAME DELETED]
- [NAME DELETED]
- [NAME DELETED]
- [NAME DELETED]

- [NAME DELETED]

- [NAME DELETED]

- [NAME DELETED]

- [NAME DELETED]

ISPHAHAN:

Special attention should be given to these reform-minded religious leaders. They can play a significant role in promoting and controlling the masses during the execution of our program. After changing the regime, these religious leaders can also contribute to the calming of society and the prevention of excesses. Furthermore, for the medium and long term period, Iran will need their cooperation in restructuring Iran's government and institutions.

A new regime in Tehran will have far reaching affects on both the country's domestic and foreign policy; as well as, it's role and influence in the Middle East and Asia. The framework of the projected changes can be defined as follows:

- Separation of State and Religion

- Democracy, Freedom and Pluralism

- Independent Judiciary and the Rule of Law

- Universal Respect for Human Rights

- Respecting the Rights of Women in every field

- Management of Iran by professionals and technocrats

- Establishment of a Free Market Economy that is Free from Corruption

- Respect of International Principles and Laws

- Return of Iran to the International community of Civilized Nations

- Condemnation and Suppression of all Terrorist Activities and Organizations; as well as, any form of subversion and interference in the affairs of other nations

- Iran would then become an important Economic Partner of the Free World—contributing its share to world prosperity, rather than absorbing and wasting resources.

Essential changes in Iran's Foreign Policy can be defined as follows:

1. Normalized relations with the United States will be the cornerstone of our new foreign policy. Relations between the two countries would again be based upon both mutual respect and interest.

2. Normalizing relations with the United States would promote normal relations with Europe.

3. While safeguarding its national interests in its relations with the Arab world, Iran would pursue a foreign policy of friendship and benevolence, and would not interfere in the affairs of other nations.

Special Areas of Iranian Foreign Policy:

1. Any nation that wants to live in peace with Israel or any other neighboring state should be able to do so. It will not be Iran's prerogative to interfere.

2. Iran shall fully cooperate with the International Community to bring peace and security to Iraq and Afghanistan; as well as, participate in their reconstruction.

REFORMERS AND RELIGIOUS LEADERS WANTING A SECULAR GOVERNMENT

[NAME DELETED]

[NAME DELETED]

[NAME DELETED]

[NAME DELETED]

[NAME DELETED]

[NAME DELETED]

[NAME DELETED]

[NAME DELETED]

[NAME DELETED]

[NAME DELETED]

A large number of younger and reformist Ayatollahs like [NAMES DELETED].

Most of the students in [NAME DELETED] reject the current government.

Student associations at the universities throughout Iran. Their leaders like [NAME DELETED] are supportive.

The majority of Town and Rural Councils were taken over by reformers in the last elections four years ago. In recent elections in Tehran, there were only 673,037 voters out of 7,000,000!!—A poor reference for the regime.

[NAME DELETED]

WHO IS WHO

CONSERVATIVE FUNDAMENTALISTS: (Hardliners)

1. Ayatollah Khameni—Supreme Leader—Religious

2. Ayatollah Mahdavi Kani—Head of the Council of "Rouha-niat e Mobarez" (Orthodox Ayatollahs)

3. Ayatollah Golpaygani—Director of the office of Khameinei

4. Ayatollah Yazdi—Former Head of Judiciary

5. Ayatollah Nouri—Former President of Parliament

6. Ayatollah H. Rouhani—General Secretary of National Security Council

7. Velayati—Former Foreign Minister

8. Kharazi—Foreign Minister

9. Asghar Oladi—Head of the Association "Motalef Islami" (Main strategist of the Hardliners)

10. Hodjat Ol Eslam Rafsandjani—Former President, Head of "Tashkhis e Maslahat", and member of "Rohaniat e Mobarez"

11. Ayatollah Janati—Head of Council of "Negahban (Council of Experts—to approve laws passed by the Parliament)

12. Ayatollah Meshkini—Head of Council of Khobregan (that chooses religious leaders)

13. Ayatollah Fallahian—Former Minister of Intelligence

14. Ayatollah Taskhiri—Head of Markaze Farhang and Etellaat Eslami

15. M. Javan Laridjani—Head of Radio and Television

16. Other important Ayatollahs: Ayatollah Amini, Ayatollah Mesbah Yazdi, Ayatollah Khazali

17. General Safavi—Head of Revolutionary Guards (R.G.)

18. General Hejasi—Head of Bassij

19. Execution arms: Naghdi, Namaki, Hosseinian, Shariati

    High placed members of the Intelligence Ministry under arrest: Pour, Mohammadi, Kazemi, Eslami (killed himself)

20. Sharoudi—Head of Judiciary and his deputy Laridjani

THE POLITICAL-RELIGIOUS ESTABLISHMENT OF THE ISLAMIC REPUBLIC

The constitution of the Islamic Republic of Iran has several power centers within its political-religious establishment.

a) the Supreme Guide, Ayatollah Khameni,

b) the President and the executive branch,

c) the Parliament,

d) Judiciary, the Council of Guardian, the Assembly of Discretion of the State,

e) the Military, Sepah, Bassij, Security Forces.

It has been assumed that these power centers would act in coordination and be complementary to each other. However since the election of Ayatollah Khatami and the start of the reform movement—due to the dual existence of both elected and appointed executives—there is continuous opposition between these power centers and Iran is facing a complete stalemate.

To understand the essence of the Islamic Republic, it is essential to have a comprehensive picture of the role of the Ayatollah Khameni, his office, his organization and the people affiliated with it. The leadership of Ayatollah Khameni is above the law and any other institution or organizations. His office acts on several different levels in the system.

A) Policy Decisions:

Ayatollah Khameni through his office makes policy decisions and issues orders for their execution. These decisions concern both domestic and foreign policy.

1) *Domestic:* Direct orders are given to the executive branch, in many cases, contradictory to Government policy. Ayatollah Khameni also paralyzes the legislative branch. He often issues a direct order, as in the case of the law regarding Freedom of the Press law. He ordered the President of the Parliament, Ayatollah Karoubi, to withdraw the submitted law. The Council of Guardian even rejects laws, already approved by Parliament. Two-thirds (⅔) of the Council is chosen by Ayatollah Khameni and Ayatollah Sharodi, who is the head of the Judiciary. Ayatollah Sharodi is himself appointed by Ayatollah Khameni and is fully faithful to him. By the mechanism of the Council of Guardian, the hardliners are paralyzing the Parliament and the executive branch (Government). The law covering foreign capital investments is an example: Whereas the Government and the Parliament had twice approved the foreign investment law, it was twice rejected by the Council blocking the Government and its basic policies. In the case of any disagreement between the Parliament, and the Council of Guardian, the final decision is made by the Assembly of Discretion of the State, again dominated by

the hardliners and its Chairman Rafsandjani. This assembly which has taken a very important role during the last two (2) years, has the final word on any important issues submitted to it.

2) *Foreign Policy*: It is also completely controlled by Ayatollah Khameni. In his office there are 508 people concerned with foreign policy. Velayati, the former Foreign Minister, Mohamad Javad Larijani, Sadgegh Kharazi (son in law of the leader), Mir Hejazi Hassan Rouhani, are the principal advisors. This group is in full opposition to the Government and the reformist majority of the Parliament.

Today, the Islamic Republic and North Korea, are the most isolated countries in the world.

B) Organizations Directly-controlled and Dependent upon the Supreme Guide:

1) *Judiciary:* As mentioned above, the head of the Judiciary, Ayatollah Sharodi was appointed by Ayatollah Khameni. Ayatollah Shahroodi has become a key player in paralyzing the Government and the Parliament by continuous arrests and trials of students, intellectuals, journalists, members of the Parliament and reformist religious. The Judiciary has become the principal tool of oppression instead of rendering justice.

2) *Radio and Television:* Radio and television are completely controlled by the Ayatollah Khameni and all programs are limited to the propaganda of the hardliners.

3) *Foundations:* Foundations report directly to Ayatollah Khameni. Among these foundations Emadad-e-Iman, 15 Khordad, and Mosta'zafan play an important role within the establishment. They mobilize large funds for

the hardliners. There is no control from the Government and they use their connections to act without regard to the laws of the country. They enjoy a monopoly while controlling both the underground economy and the black market.

4) *The military, security forces, Sepah, Basji, and the Legion of Foreigners:* The Guardians of the Revolution are disciplined and in charge of security. The Minister of Interior is only a strawman. We have within the various security and intelligence forces the same situation that in the political sphere; internecine fighting and opposition since they are too close to the different centers of power. Opposition exists mainly on the lower levels of the security apparatus where wide spread dissatisfaction can be witnessed with the leaders.

The Legion of Foreigners is disciplined and well trained. They are the "Fer de lance" of the regime for subversive activities abroad. 22,000 members from various countries compose this force. There are men from Arab countries, Afghanistan, Pakistan, Kashmir, India, Kurdistan, Turkey, Philippines, Tajikistan, Uzbekistan and several African countries. Complementary to these subversive forces are the theological schools (Madaress Elmie') in Qom, Tehran, Meshed, Isphahan, Beirut and Pakistan. During their studies, the students are brain washed, and may become future Bin Ladens in their country or in the region. There are thousands aged between 12 and 71 years, and from different countries in Asia and even Europe.

The hardliners, backed by this political setup under Ayatollah Khameni, have so far succeeded in their endeavor to block the reform movement and paralyzed the Government and the Parliament. They have successfully blocked the political–social process, and prevented the political society from opening up and allowing fundamental democratic freedom. The internal power struggle has effectively created a political stalemate and produces ever increasing social and economic problems. (The regime has proven that it cannot be reformed in any way or form) Iran will witness within a year, a change of regime. Many factors have prepared the ground for such a change.

A FORCE OF CHANGE

A) Popular Opposition:

The gap between the political–religious establishment and the people of Iran has been increasing at an accelerated speed. The population does not accept the goals and policies of the system. Its aspirations are for a better life, freedom and its cultural and its historical identity. Elections during the last year have become only a protest vote and referendum against the regime. It is fair to assume that today 80% of the population is against the regime, while amongst the youth the figure reaches 86%.

B) Governance:

There is no country in the world in which there is such an ample supply of managers, technocrats, technicians, and professionals. However, for reasons of complete control of the economy by their religious elite, there is suppression of all dissident voices and rife corruption. The nation is ruled by a group without any experience, expertise, and professionalism. For example, 84% of the members of the Foreign Ministry are from the Sepah, embassies abroad included.

C) Population:

The population of Iran has increased from 34 million in 1979 to 64 million in 2001. 65% of the population is now under 25 years. [Editor's Note: 50 percent of the population is under 20 years old.] Iran has one of the youngest populations in the world. This young population has a wide range of aspirations of reform, freedom, democracy, employment and a better life. Unable to fulfill their expectations, the regime is condemned to leave the scene. A number of economic and social indicators, as well as other trends, may reveal the depth of crises.

I—Domestic

A) Economics

Some economic indicators may underline the extent of the crisis. In our analysis, we have taken into account the growth of the population from 34 million in 1979 to 65 million in 2001.

The low level of investments, sharp drops in the Government's development budget, the reluctance of the private sector to make productive investments while the inclination towards commercial and middlemen activities have had negative impacts on the growth of GNP since the Revolution. The level of investment in Iran when compared to Saudi Arabia, Egypt, Korea, and Malasia has been negligible.

From 1979–2001 the official growth of GNP has been around .2% per year. In 1979, per capita income was $2300, today it is not more than $750. In 1979, Iran had the largest foreign exchange reserves in the region. Foreign debt had been reduced to a minimum, based on the policy of the government. In 1975/76 Iran paid back all of its international debt following the increase of its oil revenues. Today, foreign debt has soared above $20 billion, even after having rescheduled its debt several times.

The foreign exchange rate was $1 = 70 rials, today it is $1 = 8,500 rials, an increase of 1,200%. Mismanagement, corruption and the absence of a strict monetary and fiscal policy have resulted in an inflation rate well above 250% per year.

The public sector, consisting of both the government itself and several thousand state-owned enterprises, dominates the economy. While the bureaucracy is hobbled by red tape and corruption, and the poorly-managed public financial and industrial entities are kept on life support by government subsidies.

B) Industry:

Industrial production, due to lack of investments and mismanagement, reflects the shrinking of the industrial base in Iran's economy. A total of at least 1,500 factories (textile, plastics, construction and assembly) all with over 350 employees are likely to shut down their operations in the coming months due to mismanagement and financial difficulties. In many cases, salaries have not been paid since 6 months. This will add another half a million unemployed to the rapidly increasing army of unemployed.

Textile industry:

Concerning the textile industry, which is the second most important industry in the country, was flourishing in 1979 with brilliant prospects for export. Today, it is working at 37% of its capacity and 80% of the plants have been shut down. In most cases, salaries have not been paid during the last 6 months.

Oil–Gas Industry:

The oil and gas industry was one of the pillars of Iran's economy in 1979. NIOC was well know as a reliable, international company under the leadership of high level competent managers. Today, Iran's petroleum production is about 3,800,000 barrels/day. Most of the competent managers and technical staff have left the company. With no planning, lack of investment and technical stagnation, large sections of the oil–gas industry are obsolete and oil wells and fields are in danger of losing their capacity of production. According to estimates of the regime, $49 billion of investments are required to develop and save the oil and gas industry.

Internal Bank Crisis:

Meanwhile, the internal banking system has to cope with an eroded equity position due to overdue writeoffs on bad debt portfolios, such as many unsubstantiated and inadequately secured loans provided to the foundations and affiliated companies. The main cause of this development is the fact that the banks are not managed by experienced professionals, but by politically corrupt religious leaders. The banking system is currently kept afloat by periodic currency printing by the government.

Agricultural:

The Islamic Republic has always pretended that agriculture development has a high priority as it is essential to ensure the independence of the country from abroad in covering the needs of the economy. This has also been an empty slogan.

In 1979, the total area under cultivation was 10.5 million hectares. Today after 23 years it has increased only by 10%, whereas the population has increased from 34 million in 1979 to 64 million in 2001. Production of rice, wheat, barely, which was 12 million tons in 1979, has only increased to 14 million. Annual imports of these products, which in 1979 amounted to 4 million, now stand at more than 10 million.

Production of cotton, the basis of Iran's textile industry, has dropped from 550,000 tons in 1979 to 350,000 tons per year.

Infrastructure:

To have any idea of the desolate situation of Iran's infrastructure here are some self-telling figures. The roads in Iran are often called "roads of blood"! In 2001 there were 20,000 accidents with 15,000 killed and 87,000 injured— making Iran's highways the most dangerous in the world. In March 24, 2004 a new record was established with 122 dead and 1,800 injured in a single day! The situation of ports, shipping, airports and civil airlines are worse than one can imagine.

Tourism:

With the expansion of the tourism industry in the world, Iran has with its ancient history all that is necessary to develop its tourism industry on a large scale and enjoy a source of substantial revenues. Unfortunately, by its policies, the regime has in fact written off the potentials of tourism in Iran. Today, the only well-known tourists in Iran are members of Taliban and Al Qaeda.

The data dramatizes how a working economic system, which by corruption and mismanagement, has been plundered of all of its wealth and assets since 1979. This group for the sake of its own interest has monopolized all economic centers with the help of its corrupted "Homme de main," and has left only a dated economy which today is in total ruin.

C) Social

Income Structure:

The destruction of Iran's once booming economy since the revolution has had far reaching social consequences. In the absence of economic growth corresponding to Iran's potential and its increase in population, the income structure reflects a very dangerous picture. Iran is facing slow economic growth, a low level of income and a high concentration of wealth. Iran's strong middle class has been driven toward the lower income groups of society. Today only 15% of the people own 50% of the country's wealth, while the top 10% of income earners consume 31% of the available goods and services. The share of the bottom 10% is only 1.5%. 47% of the population now lives in poverty.

Unemployment:

The government has completely failed to address unemployment. Iran's unemployment rate (hidden unemployment included) is currently around 30%. Iran is among the 5 countries with the highest rates of unemployment. Before 1979, Iran was one of the largest importers of foreign labor, mainly from Asian countries. Today, we find Iranian labor everywhere: Japan, Canada, Europe and the Middle East.

The combination of a young population and high unemployment is a "time bomb" that no society can afford.

Education System:

The education system is another aspect of the social crisis. The education system faces a declining level of education and an absence of hope for students to play a positive role in society. There are around 18 million students enrolled in schools and universities. Of this number, there are around 600,000 students at public universities and other institutes, and 700,000 students at the "Islamic Azad Universities." These Islamic Universities have become a headache for the education system. Without standards of control, and in most cases, without qualified teachers, they are pouring out students with certificates having no value, and in most cases not accepted to get a job. These universities have created only expectations and despair. Recent studies show that suicide and drug overdose cases are high among these students.

To staff the schools throughout the country, there are 1,800,000 teachers in Iran. 437,000 of these exist in the central province of Tehran. Due to low salaries and miserable conditions of life, the teachers have started to demonstrate in many towns, and the movement is gaining momentum.

Emigration and Brain Drain:

With no future in Iran, emigration is on the rise. There are 4,300,000 Iranians abroad, of whom a large number are doctors, scientists, engineers, chemists, experts. In this respect, Iran occupies a very high position in the U.S.A. At NASA, 17 top managers and technicians are from Iran. Each year about 20,000 of the best minds are leaving Iran. During 2001, there were 186,000 applications of the country's elite to emigrate. Not included are those who leave illegally.

Prisons:

According to a United Nations report Iran has the most prisoners that are journalists, politicians and social scientists. According to Ayatollah Shahroodi, Head of Judiciary, there are 917,000 prisoners in Iran. 107,000 of them are considered political prisoners, including a large number of students, teachers, politicians, and political activists below 30 years of age.

Drugs and Prostitution:

Compared to its population, Iran has one of the highest percentage of drug addicts. Last month in Tehran, 18,600 young people died of drug overdoses. According to official figures during 2000, 800,000 drug addicts were arrested. Total users within Iran are estimated to be at 2,500,000.

In the past, the Philippines and Thailand were known for their prostitution. Today Iran is also known for its prostitutes in the country and abroad, mainly in Turkey and Emirates. There is also a large available supply of body parts, like kidneys, livers, etc. currently available for sale in Iran.

Health:

The public health situation is deteriorating rapidly in Iran. There is a chronic shortage of medicines and health facilities for the population at large. Hospitals are lacking equipment and professional people. 80% of the medicines must be purchased on the black market. Old endemic diseases are now reappearing. The social developments tend to reveal the extent to what the social structure of the Iranian society is suffering from the policies of the regime. These policies are completely alien to Iran's society and culture.

II—INTERNATIONAL CONSTELLATION

In addition to the domestic crisis, the international events of the last six (6) months have become challenges for the regime in Iran. The immobility of the regime to change and moderate its foreign policy toward the United States, will be the cause of its own demise. Recent events have been crystallized to three (3) issues between Iran and the United States.

- Production of Arms of Mass Destruction (WMD) by Iran

- Making of Chemical and Biological Arms

- Interference in Neighboring States

In addition to the number of official Russian nuclear technicians, there are 375 more experts with private contracts from Russia, ex-CIS countries, Serbia, and North Korea working in Iran for the production of nuclear arms. Iran is also building nuclear power stations at the seaside in the south. Not only is obsolete technology used, but it is also a mixture of Russian and older European technology. The effect of an accident or sabotage there would have worse consequences than Chernobyl, since these facilities are close to the neighboring Arab countries in the south of the Gulf.

MEMO

SUBJECT: Meeting with "Ali" April 25, 2003

Congressman Curt Weldon, Vice Chairman of the House
Armed Services Committee, and Dr. Peter Vincent Pry of Mr.
Weldon's staff, met with a potential intelligence source, pseu-
donym "Ali" on April 25, 2003, at 4:00 PM, at the Renaissance
Hotel in La Defense, 60 Jardin Boulevard Circulaire, Paris,
France. Ali refused the services of a professional stenographer
hired for the meeting through the hotel, fearing such services
might be compromised by French intelligence.

[PARAGRAPH DELETED]

MEETING ABSTRACT

[PARAGRAPH DELETED]

[PARAGRAPH DELETED]

Ali said that on Tuesday (April 22) he received an unexpected
call from the French Ministry of Interior asking for an immediate meeting. This request was surprising, Ali said, because he had
no contact with the French Interior Ministry for 8–9 years. Ali
met for 40 minutes with a French Interior Ministry agent responsible for Iranian matters at a café. According to Ali, the French
agent asked Ali to disclose his Iranian sources who were alleging
that the government of Iran planned to assassinate former President George Bush. Ali said he refused to reveal his sources
because this would destroy his sources and Ali's credibility. Ali
said that current French intelligence tends to discount his credibility because they view him as a survivor of the Shah's old
regime, and do not know about his sources and connections cultivated over the last 20 years. He said French intelligence used to
understand that Ali is well connected to the current Iranian gov-

ernment, but that those who knew him well in French intelligence have retired. Ali said that yesterday (April 24) he called a friend in the German Embassy to find out if Ali's allegations about an assassination plot against George Bush Sr. Had been passed to German intelligence. Ali said that he was told by his friend that German intelligence had been informed of Ali's allegation about an assassination plot against former President Bush.

Ali said he was never approached by the Central Intelligence Agency to discuss his allegations.

Ali claims that the Iranian government believes "old" Bush is the real "power behind the throne" of the current President, not "young" George Bush. Ali claims Tehran believes that Washington's allegedly anti-Iranian policies are being driven by "old" Bush. Accordingly, Iran plans to assassinate the former President, and believes this will be less challenging than assassinating the sitting President, because "old" Bush is less well protected.

Ali said that sensitive information about the government of Iran is conveyed to him usually in face-to-face meetings with contacts in places outside Iran, like Geneva, Switzerland. He said his Iranian connections are the product of 20 years of working against the present government of Iran.

Ali said that when George Bush Sr. Wanted to be President, there was an investigation into allegations that President Reagan asked Iran not to free the U.S. Embassy hostages. Ali said these allegations were a "big lie" based on a "stupid book" that someone had written. He said a U.S. Senate Committee and the CIA talked to him for 5 hours at the U.S. Embassy in Paris about these allegations. According to Ali, he helped rebut these allegations by pointing out that a meeting that supposedly took place in Madrid between U.S. officials and an Iranian Mullah is easily explained by the fact that the Mullah was "a playboy." The

Mullah, according to Ali, was in Madrid not to meet with Reagan officials, but for pleasure. Ali, when queried, said he did not know who Faith Whittlesey was in connection with "Irangate."

Ali said that his sources inform him that the government of Iran has made a strategic decision to destabilize Afghanistan and Iraq, to thwart U.S. plans to establish stable governments in these countries. Iran sees its own survival at risk if the U.S. succeeds in establishing stable democracies in these countries, according to Ali. Accordingly, Iran has provided refuge to Osama Bin Laden in a safe-house near Tehran, located in the northern suburb of Pasdaran, Ali said. He said the safe-house is owned by the Iranian Oil Company. Ali alleges that the safe-house is equipped with secure telephone lines, formerly belonging to the Shah's SAVAK, and is protected by Iranian Revolutionary Guards.

Ali said that his information on Bin Laden's presence and location in Iran was not based on information from [NAME DELETED] but from his own special sources. [SENTENCE DELETED]

Ali said he "was never misled" by his sources and is fully confident in their information. Ali claimed these same sources provided him with information that Saddam Hussein had survived the U.S. attack targeting him at a Baghdad restaurant merely 30 minutes after the event. According to Ali, these sources told him Saddam left the restaurant early, in a Russian vehicle, that took him to an airport.

Ali alleges that one of his three best sources is a senior military officer, a general, serving on [DELETED] staff. He said he has received 7 written reports from his sources in January.

Ali claimed that his information about Iran's atomic bomb program was from two reliable sources, including the general and

[DELETED]. According to Ali, Iran has decided to follow a policy similar to North Korea's, and crash on acquiring an atomic bomb, allocating $10 billion to accelerate the program. Ali claims Iran is making rapid progress toward developing an A-bomb. According to Ali, Iran will have enough nuclear material to build an atomic bomb by July–August 2003. Ali said Iran plans to conduct its first test of an atomic bomb in September 1–17, 2003.

Ali alleges Iran has made three trips to North Korea through China to negotiate the purchase of an atomic bomb. According to Ali, Iran has offered North Korea $3 billion for one atomic bomb, or $2 billion for enough nuclear material for one atomic bomb, and 10 North Korean experts to help. He said Iran's objective is to gen an A-bomb before mid-September.

Ali offered to buy intelligence for the United States from Iranian officials. According to Ali, most Iranian officials realize the regime is about to collapse, and are willing to trade state secrets for personal security. Ali noted that in Iran's last election, with 7 million voters in Tehran, only 673,000 voters participated. Ali noted that other signs of regime collapse in Iran are the escalating cost of living, growing civil disobedience among the young, and growing poverty so great that the sale of Iranian virgins to Arab countries has become Iran's second biggest sources of income. Ali provided materials from Iran student newspapers and dissidents that he alleges demonstrate the regime is in the verge of collapse ("within 3 months of revolution"), and will face a serious uprising from dissidents on July 18, 2003.

Ali offered to serve as a conduit for bribing Iranian officials for intelligence on such issues as: financing of terrorism; atomic bomb program; Osama Bin Laden; and Russian ties to Iran. Ali claimed he could deliver intelligence on these and other issues within 120 days of our request, "or our money back." In this connection, Ali said he could get documents signed by high-ranking Iranian officials ("Khomeini and Khatami") proving that Iran has financed and coordinated the establishment of a "terrorist super-organization" that incorporates Hezballah, Hamas, Islamic Jihad and other terror groups. Ali claims Iran is working on a terrorist operation targeting the United States that "will be worse than September 11." He said a Mr. Hekmatyar is a key Iranian terrorist.

Ali alleges that Iran is helping high officials of Iraq escape. He claims 136 top Iraqi officials have fled to Sudan via Iran. Ali said 3 Iraqi generals have found refuge in Shiraz, Iran. He said Iran has moved two training camps for terrorists to Mamassani in the Gasshqai region (near where his family owned land) and between Nour (sp) and Kazerun (sp). He said the Mullahs have started a television station at Kermanshah on the Iraqi border that is intended to "mobilize the sheiks" against the Americans. Ali offered to provide the exact coordinates of the television station that he suggested should be destroyed by cruise missile attack.

Ali claimed the Iranian programs for nuclear, chemical, and biological weapons are more advanced than the Iraqi programs. Ali said Iran has 300–400 missiles with ranges greater 1,000 kilometers. [SENTENCE DELETED].

On Sunday, April 27, 2003, Ali called Dr. Pry at the Renaissance Hotel to say that Ali had just been informed by one of his best sources in the Iranian government that: 1) the Iranian government had made a decision to execute Yasser Arafat in the near future ("within 20 days") because he had become a liability; and 2) Iran had acquired a missile from North Korea having a range greater than 3,500 kilometers.

3

ALI REPORTS

27–29 April 2003

" I he regime in Iran is poison to the democratic stability of
  the region!"

—Ali

IN THE REPORTS THAT FOLLOW, Ali offers "within 120 days" to buy
information from his sources on a broad range of topics vital to U.S.
national security. The CIA turned him down.

Some highlights from these reports:

- "Iran has decided to follow a policy similar to North Korea: to have
  the bomb, and being in a position of power, to oblige the United
  States to negotiate." This warning, ignored by the intelligence community at the time, is precisely what the Bush administration suspects Iran is plotting today.

- Tehran makes a strategic decision that democracy in Iraq and
  Afghanistan threatens theocracy in Iran, and so democracy in these
  countries must be destroyed at all costs.

- More on the "super-terrorist organization" created by the Committee of Nine.

Dear Curt:

With financial assistance from CIA for my sources in Iran, I can within 120 days provide the following information:

1) Financial network for financing terrorism (with documents)

2) Atom bomb program

3) Bin Laden

4) Cooperation of extremists (Mohtaschamipour)

5) Emad Mognie–Anisss Nagash; Morteza Rezai intelligence of Sepah

6) Sepah in Pakistan

7) Information and situation and system

8) Arrange meeting with VIP in Iran

9) What project they have in Iran

10) Change of regime blue print

11) What happens next in Iran.

Best regards,
Ali
April 27, 2003

Dear Curt:

Political aspect.

Iran has decided to follow a policy similar to North Korea: to have the bomb, and being in a position of power, to oblige the United States to negotiate.

Technical aspect.

1) Production of the nuclear product at Iran's facilities is in progress. It was planned that the quantity of nuclear material necessary would be available in the second half of May. Latest reports show that the quantity required would be available July–August.

2) Experimental test has been planned 1–17 September, it would be Iran's first atomic explosion. However Khameni has told Aghazadeh he can have a budget of $10 billion to accelerate the program.

3) International aspect. There have been several trips of Pasdaran to North Korea. There are two proposals on the table.

   To North Korea:

   a) Iran would buy an atomic bomb against $3 billion (Money in Shanghai Bank)

   b) Iran would pay $2 billion for the product to make a bomb and the availability of ten North Korean experts.

Absolute Priority: Prevent Iran to have the bomb by any of these possibilities.

Best regards,
Ali
April 27, 2003

Dear Curt:

The constitution of Iran provides for several principal power centers. Since the start of the reform movement Iran is facing complete stalemate. This is due to the dual existence of elected and appointed officials and the fact that the leadership of Khameni is above law and order.

Khameni initiates domestic and foreign policies. He controls the Judiciary, the Council of Guardians and the Assembly is at the discretion of the state. Khameni controls all security forces, the media and religious–financial foundations. The political stalemate is aggravating every day the social–economic crisis. The failure of the reform movement is considered by the majority of the society as the proof that the regime cannot be reformed. The aspirations of the population for regime change was shown most demonstrably in the recent elections for town councils, which became a referendum against the regime.

For example, in Tehran there were 7 million potential voters. Only 673,370 votes were cast, less than 1%! There is a strongly increasing consensus within the society for:

a) separation of the state from the religion

b) democracy, freedom, pluralism, human rights, respect of women's rights

c) management of the country by professionals and technocrats

d) establishment of free market economy

e) return of Iran among the international community of civilized countries.

In governmental organizations the regime is regarded as doomed. The main concern of the officials is their future.

International events since September 11 have crystallized several issues between Iran and the United States:

a) Production of weapons of mass destruction by Iran

b) Iran's opposition to peace in the Middle East and its support of terrorism in the region

c) Iran's subversive activities against the United States in Afghanistan and support to Al-Quaeda in Iran

d) The victory of the United States in Iraq and the presence of American troops

e) American support for democracy in the Middle East

With any concession on these basic issues, the regime would lose it's credibility and its foundation would destabilize. Consequently, Iran's regime fears and seeks to prevent the same fate as Afghanistan and Iraq, imposed by a popular pro-American uprising in Iran. French journalists recently reporting on the situation in Iran wrote: "In no other town in the world has the American dream a comparable aspiration...expecting to become reality with the arrival of the Marines." Iran has taken the path to prevent by all means stable governments in Afghanistan and Iraq. The regime in Iran is poison to the democratic stability of the region!

A quick change of regime can be considered as essential for the stability of Afghanistan and Iraq. It would also prevent Iran from becoming with its program of missiles and atomic bombs, the challenge "a la North Korea."

Best regards,
Ali
April 29, 2003

Dear Curt:

1) Khameni has issued an order to kill Arafat and any help to him in any form should be stopped. He is accused of promoting "American peace." As I told you in our meeting in Paris, a unified super-organization of terrorism has been created recently on the order of Khameni to target American and Israeli targets. This organization includes: Hezballah–Hamas–Jihad Islamic–Ansar Islam–Sepah Badr, Al Qaeda and the foreign legions of Sepah. Tehran believes that Yasser Arafat's death would strengthen this organization. Furthermore Tehran believes that Arafat's assassination would create turmoil in the region and undermine for the time being the peace discussions. In addition, Arafat is accused of giving information on the Iranian involvement in terrorism.

2) The region around Dehloran on the Iran–Iraq border has been left open by Iran, so that Iraqi's can fly to Iran.

3) Ayatollah Mohammed Bagher Al Hakim , 63 is expected to move to Iraq in the next 60 days. Bagher Hakim is son of Muhssen Hakim, Grand Ayatollah of the 1960's. After Saddam tortured him and murdered much of his family, Hakim the son escaped to Iran, spending the past two decades heading up the Supreme Council for the Islamic Revolution in Iraq and the strong Badre Brigade, trained and armed by Iran's Republican Guards.

To prepare Hakim's return a campaign of propaganda is being proposed and large printing facilities for leaflets, etc. put in place.

The battle for Najaf is as much theological as political. Khameni is aspiring to become leader of Shiites. He tries to make Ghom the principal religious center of Shiitism, based on the principle of "Velayate Faghih," the rule of the clergy imposed by Khomeni after the Islamic revolution in 1979.

Whereas Najaf holds that clerics should advise but not govern; clerics have traditionally been encouraged to embrace "ijtihad"—independent judgment—rather than follow leaders blindly. The recently slain Sheikh Syed Abdul Majeed Khoie espoused this stand of Islam. Najaf's current Grand Ayatollah, Ali Sistani, 73, is the most revered Shiite authority in Iraq. Given the choice Iraqi Shiites choose Arab Iraq over Persian Iran.

4) A delegation of several generals has gone to Turkmenistan and signed several contracts. From there they have gone to Turkey. On the order of Khameni, they have shown themselves in their discussions with the Turkish authorities most cooperative and Iran has decided to spend lavishly money in Turkey to strengthen its influence.

5) Iran is going to experiment with a missile in the next weeks. Iran has several missiles with a range of 3500 km.

6) I gave you a memorandum on Iran's atom bomb program. I am trying to get you the information you asked me. As you emphasized yourself this is of utmost importance. Tehran believes firmly that with regard to its program of missiles and atomic bomb, Israel deserves no future in the region, and Iran is concentrating more and more on a second 11 September attack against the United States. We shall try our best to obtain information on this project and inform you before hand.

7) Large finance has been allocated and is being spent to support leftists opposed to the United States in Europe.

8) Iran is firmly decided to intervene in the American presidential election next year. With the cooperation of 3 businessmen

in Los Angeles, they expect to help, against President Bush, Clinton's party and the candidate that Khameni calls in meetings the "playboy."

Best regards,
Ali
April 29, 2003

4

ALI REPORTS

1–18 May 2003

"Concerns terrorists actions in the United States: An attack
   against a nuclear reactor by a plane to be hijacked in
   Canada."

—Ali

AMONG THE MAY 2003 REPORTS, of particular interest is the report of
May 17. Here, Ali's sources on the Committee of Nine disclose a terrorist plot, managed from Tehran, to hijack an airliner in Canada and
crash it into a nuclear reactor in the United States. Ali later learned
that the target was the Seabrook Nuclear Reactor, surrounded by
more than one million people, and only forty miles from Boston.

The objective was to inflict a blow more catastrophic than the attacks
of September 11 by inflicting perhaps hundreds of thousands of casualties from radiation poisoning, and rendering one of the United
States' most populous areas uninhabitable.

Terrorists would not expect to trigger an atomic explosion by crashing an airliner into a nuclear reactor. Instead, the aim is to penetrate
the reactor dome and cause a fire that would vaporize the uranium
fuel rods, creating a poisonous radioactive plume, which would contaminate thousands of square miles. Alternatively, terrorists could
crash a plane into the reactor building containing spent fuel rods—
which is not protected by a thick concrete dome—and achieve the
same result.

Could the terrorists achieve their goal? According to a Congressional Research Service (CRS) report, *Nuclear Power Plants: Vulnerability to Terrorist Attack* (September 17, 2004): "Nuclear power plants were designed to withstand hurricanes, earthquakes, and other extreme events, but attacks by large airliners loaded with fuel, such as those that crashed into the World Trade Center and Pentagon, were not contemplated when design requirements were determined." CRS notes, "Nuclear industry spokespersons" have offered the assurance that, "Relatively small, low-lying nuclear power plants are difficult targets for attacks." However, the CRS also notes that the "U.S. NRC [Nuclear Regulatory Commission] is considering studies of additional measures to mitigate the effects of an aircraft crash."

Contrary to "nuclear industry spokespersons," Israel had no difficulty attacking Iraq's Osirak Nuclear Reactor on July 7, 1981. Israel penetrated the Osirak reactor's massive dome using simple, unguided "bombs" of solid iron. The Israelis used no high explosives against Osirak precisely because they did not want to start a radioactive fire that would wreak mass destruction on Iraqi civilians.

The terrorists of September 11 successfully targeted both World Trade Center buildings and the Pentagon. Nuclear reactors are big targets too. Recently, the *Washington Post* reported that, "Three and a half years after the September 11, 2001, attacks, the government has failed to address the risk that a passenger plane flying at high speeds could be deliberately crashed into a commercial nuclear plant, setting off fires and dispersing large amounts of radiation, a long-awaited report by the National Academy of Sciences has concluded." ("Nuclear Plants Are Still Vulnerable, Panel Says," *Washington Post,* April 7, 2005.) Authors of the National Academy of Sciences report *Safety and Security of Commercial Spent Nuclear Fuel Storage* said that, where commercial nuclear reactors are concerned, "There are currently no requirements in place to defend against the kinds of larger-scale, premeditated, skillful attacks that were carried out on September 11, 2001." Further, the *Post* reported that National Academy of Science officials "battled the government for months to make their declassified conclusions public—and the version released yesterday charged that federal secrecy edicts designed to keep information from terrorists were paradoxically hurting efforts to defend against such attacks."

Interestingly, the Seabrook Nuclear Reactor has an unclassified website with excellent aerial photographs and map coordinates of the reactor dome and other facilities. The Seabrook website provides details on the design of the reactor dome, "a unique dome-within-a dome design, which is made of 6.5 feet of steel-reinforced concrete." The Osirak dome was thicker. These website details on Seabrook's dome design, unclassified and available to anyone, would be of great interest to a targeteer. Professional military targeteers tell me that, if a good engineer knows how something is designed, they can figure out how to destroy it. The website also boasts that the Seabrook Reactor is invulnerable to attack.

If terrorists attacked the Seabrook Nuclear Reactor successfully, the consequences would almost certainly be worse than the Chernobyl nuclear accident that happened in Ukraine on April 26, 1986. Seabrook has more nuclear material than was at Chernobyl. Seabrook's location, compared to the Chernobyl Nuclear reactor, is in an area of higher population density.

The fire at Chernobyl was the worst nuclear accident in history. The plume from Chernobyl dispersed 50 tons of radioactive dust over 140,000 square miles of Belarus, Ukraine, and Russia. This is an area over twice the size of all the New England states. The radioactive plume from Chernobyl covered an area equivalent to the states of New Hampshire, Massachusetts, Vermont, Maine, Connecticut, Rhode Island, New Jersey, New York, and most of Pennsylvania. Living in these nine states are over 48,000,000 people.

An estimated 4.9 million people were exposed to dangerous radiation levels from the Chernobyl nuclear accident. In addition, about 700,000 emergency and clean-up workers—we call them "first responders" in the United States—were acutely exposed to radioactivity.

Radiation poisoning kills people slowly and by indirect means, through cancers and other effects. So calculating the number of casualties from radiation poisoning generally, or specifically from the Chernobyl disaster, is controversial. In general, in a Chernobyl-type disaster, if people living within twenty miles of the nuclear reactor are not promptly evacuated or sheltered from the plume, they could receive exposure to acute levels of radiation and die within a few weeks or months. But the vast majority of fatalities would occur much more slowly than this. People living hundreds of miles away who are exposed to the plume can, typically five to fifteen years after exposure, contract fatal cancers. Babies, children, and young adults are most at risk.

The best guess by the Liquidators' Committee—a panel of experts convened by Russia, Ukraine, and Belarus—is that Chernobyl has killed 100,000 people so far. Radioactivity from Chernobyl has rendered thousands of square miles of once productive territory dangerous to live in or uninhabitable. Since 1986, more than 300,000 people have been evacuated from the towns and villages near Chernobyl.

Seventeen years after the Chernobyl nuclear accident, the United Nations report *The Human Consequences of the Chernobyl Nuclear Accident* (January 25, 2002) found that the catastrophe has still not ended:

> The affected population—those exposed to radioactive fallout, remaining in the affected areas, or forced to relocate—continue to face disproportionate suffering in terms of health, social conditions, and economic opportunity. Hundreds of thousands of people have been evacuated from the most severely affected areas. Many have found it difficult to adapt and continue to face serious psychological, economic and social problems. The process of evacuation has now virtually ceased and only a small number of people continue to live in the most polluted areas. However, some tens of thousands

remain in areas polluted to a level of between 15 and 40 curies per square kilometer.

The radioactive fallout from the Chernobyl accident contaminated large territories in all three countries affecting life in rural communities for decades to come. Agriculture and forestry are forbidden in wide areas. Poverty forces many people to eat contaminated berries, mushrooms, game and fish, to feed contaminated hay to their cattle and to burn radioactively contaminated firewood in their stoves. Many of those living in the affected areas are ignorant of the risks that they face, or have adopted a fatalistic attitude.

Plume analysis of a successful terrorist attack on the Seabrook Nuclear Reactor indicates that radiation poisoning could kill some 200,000 people. This is a conservative estimate that assumes the radioactive plume does not travel very far inland or down the coasts, and is mostly blown by wind out to sea. A less benign scenario calculates a radioactive plume from the Seabrook Nuclear Reactor could result in as many as 800,000 fatalities.

As in the Chernobyl case, hundreds or thousands of square miles of territory would be uninhabitable or dangerous to live in. Dangerous levels of radiation could persist for three hundred years.

I notified the intelligence community of Ali's warning about a terrorist plot to attack the Seabrook Nuclear Reactor immediately upon receiving this report. Three months later, a terrorist cell was arrested in Canada apparently preparing to hijack an airliner for an attack against a nuclear reactor in the United States. The terrorists were taking pilot training, practice-flying over a Canadian nuclear reactor, probably in order to sharpen their targeting skills against Seabrook.

There has been a lot of attention paid in the left-wing press in Canada and the United States to the fact that none of these terrorists—the so-called "Toronto 19"—were actually tried or convicted for terrorism. The Royal Canadian Mounted Police and Canada's

Public Security and Anti-Terrorism unit have been unfairly derided, both by the press and Muslim activist groups in Canada, as "keystone cops" and "racists" for supposedly falsely accusing the "Toronto 19" of terrorism.

Responding to these charges in 2004, an internal investigation found that the Canadian police and anti-terrorist agents had acted properly in arresting the "Toronto 19." Moreover, they had good reason, based on publicly known facts from the anti-terrorism operation "Project Thread."

- Members of the "Toronto 19" were all single Muslim males eighteen to thirty-three years old from Pakistan, with the exception of one Indian. Significantly, Ali told us the terrorist cell in Canada plotting to attack the Seabrook Nuclear Reactor would be mostly Pakistani or Saudi, not Iranian, as the Committee of Nine did not want the plot traced back to Tehran.

- Most of the "Toronto 19" were from, or had connections to, Pakistan's Punjab province, noted for Sunni extremism, and had studied at the same madrassa, a school notorious for teaching militant Islam.

- All were in Canada illegally, on fake student visas obtained with phony documents from Ottawa Business College, a front operation supporting illegal immigration into Canada. All entered Canada before September 11, 2001, the last just six days before al Qaeda's attack on the World Trade Center and the Pentagon.

- Like the September 11 terrorists, the "Toronto 19" lived together in groups, kept to themselves, did not attend classes, pursued no other occupations, and lacked visible means of support. Yet, with no identifiable source of income, one of them had over $40,000 in the bank.

- One member of the "Toronto 19" was associated with the Global Relief Organization, identified by the FBI and the United Nations as a terrorist front operation that raises funds for al Qaeda and other terrorist groups.

- The fire department made repeated emergency calls to one of the apartments used by the group, where it is suspected they were mixing and testing explosives, similar to a terrorist cell discovered in England, which was caught because of their repeated apartment fires.

- Members of the "Toronto 19" traveled from Canada to the United States, apparently to reconnoiter targets. Members of the group collected schematics of airliners, firearms, and important buildings.

- Members of the "Toronto 19" were highly curious about nuclear matters. They cultivated associates known to have access to nuclear gauges and are suspected of stealing a nuclear gauge in Toronto. These devices, commonly used in construction, contain a small amount of radioactive cesium-137, a potential ingredient for a "dirty bomb."

- Two members of the "Toronto 19" were arrested for trying to penetrate the perimeter of the Pickering Nuclear Reactor at 4:00 in the morning. They claimed they wanted to walk on the beach.

- One member of the group was training to get a commercial pilot's license for multi-engine jets, and practiced flying over the Pickering Nuclear Reactor.

All of the evidence linking the "Toronto 19" to terrorism—three vanloads of documents and thirty computers seized from the group by the Public Security and Anti-Terrorism investigators—may never be publicly disclosed. Canada elected to deport most of the "Toronto 19" as illegal immigrants, rather than prosecute them as terrorists.

Why were the "Toronto 19" not prosecuted as terrorists? The United States' war on terrorism, and attempts to toughen Canada's anti-terrorism laws, are highly unpopular in Canada. The Canadian government may have feared that a trial would have alienated its liberal political base. Prosecutors may have judged, despite compelling circumstantial evidence, that convicting the "Toronto 19" of terrorism would have been difficult in such a negative political climate. Finally, in order to convict the "Toronto 19" of terrorism, the Canadian government would have to disclose their intelligence sources and methods, including any links to the CIA and the FBI. Such disclosures could cripple future anti-terror operations, and links to Washington's war on terrorism would be politically damaging to the Canadian government.

Ironically, seven of the "Toronto 19" have applied for refugee status in Canada, a lengthy legal proceeding, which the government must grant under Canadian law, on the grounds they will be persecuted or executed as terrorists in their own countries. Can there be any wonder that Iran's Committee of Nine, according to Ali, still considers Canada as an ideal base for mounting terrorist attacks against the United States?

If the story of Canada's "Project Thread" is ever fully told, I believe the intelligence provided by Ali on the "Toronto 19" will prove to have been decisive in stopping the attack on the Seabrook Nuclear Reactor. As can be inferred from later Ali missives, the attack on Seabrook was probably scheduled for November 2003, just three months after the "Toronto 19" were arrested.

Even after this intelligence miracle, which probably saved thousands of American lives, the CIA still refused to work with Ali.

Dear Curt:

1) There was again a meeting between Khameni and Bin Laden in Tehran. Please note, I have emphasized several times that he is in Tehran. My source informs me that, they are considering a change of location.

2) To strengthen the loyalty of his forces Khameni has issued the following order:

   a) a new car should be given to them

   b) a mobile phone with no charges

   c) their salary to be increased by 300%

   d) their holidays and expenses will be taken care of.

   The number of these privileged forces are 5,000.

3) In my report of April 21, I had mentioned that Khameni had decided that there should be no dissent and any opposition would be suppressed; in such a way that there would be only one center of power under his leadership.

   During the last days his order is being executed without delay and limitations. Arrests and trials are carried out. The new Mayor of Tehran is the deputy of the mafia terrorist organization of Ansar Hezballah. The newspaper of the council of Tehran has been taken over by the extremists and the head of Guardian of the Revolution has declared yesterday "that from now it is the duty of the Guardian of Revolution to ensure that all members of Parliament are loyal." Khoiniah, a leading reformist, has been summoned to the court. The name of Velayati, the former doctor foreign minister and who is today Khameni's advisor for foreign policy, is mentioned as future President of Republic to replace Khameni. The judge Said Mortazani, who is judge of the revolutionary cause, who has issued all the condemnation of reformers, has become Prosecutor of Tehran.

4) *Iran has long range missiles (3500 km).* Iran has changed the missile name, but they are in fact Taepodong missiles from North Korea. Iran has taken delivery of *11* missiles. Iran had asked for *90* missiles, but our source believes it would get only another nine.

5) Iran has created an Arab speaking army corps. It has 11,000 members. The 600 agents, who have been sent to Iraq for subversion, are members of this army corps. They all have Arabic identity cards. This army corps is cooperating with the army corps of Basij.

6) The Foreign Ministry expert, we mentioned in previous report and who is a Khameni man, has written in his latest report, "the British Foreign Minister is a man with whom we can have a dialogue and he is decent." Whereas the British Defense Minister is crazy and even worse than Rumsfeld! This Foreign Ministry expert submits a weekly report to Khameni.

7) Close intelligence sources of Khameni have reported to him, learned in information and interrogations of Iraqi's who have fled Iraq, that Iraq has obtained two payments from Sheikh of Dubai, one $1million and a second one of $2 million for his cooperation with Iraq. Khameni has responded "he is an Islamist and cooperation should be strengthened with him."

8) The events in *Fallujah* during the last few days, where some people have been killed, is a classic example of Iran's Islamic Republic behavior. We have witnessed before the Iranian revolution in 1979: provoke security forces, have some people killed, use their mourning and funeral service to exasperate emotions and create continuous trouble.

9) In our last report we have mentioned that 3 high ranking Iraqis have fled to Iran. Now our source informs us that the number may be higher. We are trying to find out their names.

Please note that time is running out. We have to move. It will be a very hot summer!

Best regards,
Ali
May 1, 2003

Dear Friend:

For many years I have had no contact whatsoever with the French Ministry of Interior.

After I gave you information about a possible terrorist attack against President George Bush, Sr.—which you passed on to CIA and the Secret Service, I got a telephone call. The gentleman said he is from France's Ministry of the Interior, the French equivalent of the FBI, and wanted to see me. I was pleased to have a chance to expose my point of view on the catastrophic situation in Iran and said we could meet in a few days, so that I have a chance to prepare my files. His reply was he has called me about a terrorist threat and he would appreciate to see me without delay. I agreed.

He started by telling me that I had given information on a terrorist project, and he was keen to know my source. My answer was:

a) I have been in politics for years and years, and my contacts are by no means limited.

b) For information I rely only on information coming from *inside* Iran. Information coming from opposition sources abroad, have as far as I am concerned, no value. (He agreed.)

c) Even information coming from Iran must come from the councils of power.

d) Consequently when I give information like the one you are referring to, I am convinced that it is right and coming from the right source.

e) The criteria that I apply in giving information are: I must be convinced it is just; it must be effective, by effective, I mean *harm the Mullahs and the regime,*

f) Yourself being officers of intelligence, you can understand that I shall never reveal my sources of intelligence.

The rest of the meeting was generalities and mostly I tried to explain to him that events related to the Shiites in Iraq was the fight between Ghom and Najaf and Ghom had no chance to win the fight. We agreed to meet again so that I can share my information with them about Iran.

I came out of the meeting persuaded that the information had been given to them by the American CIA and not by the fact that they may have listened to my phone used other eavesdropping techniques.

To be sure, I contacted my source at the German embassy and asked him to find out if the information had also been made available to Germany. The next day I got confirmation

Second meeting

It lasted 2 hours. The situation in Iran and Iraq was discussed.

When I started to tell him that the regime is doomed, his answer was, one cannot be sure, as for long years this has been said by some people. I replied the situation is today different and gave him my reasons. It is interesting to note that he finally agreed with me that the differences between Iran and the United States are so basic that there cannot be any agreement between the two countries. Consequently, Iran will oppose the United States, and the United States shall not be ready to accept Iran's subversion in Afghanistan and Iraq.

I emphasized that I am not talking about any military action against Iran. The solution is in Iran itself. In the now favorable international constellation there would be a pro-American uprising in Iran. When I mentioned that I would be back in before 6 months, he said he would be pleased for me. I got the impression he was sincere.

I started to discuss French policy towards Iran. He said Iran is a very important country, which has a role to play, a role in the region; and one has to keep talking to Iran. My answer was maybe basically what you are saying might be right, but today this is completely *depasse'*. The statement of France's Foreign Ministry in Tehran, a few days ago in Tehran, that reforms are moving ahead in Iran, is proof that he doesn't know what he is talking about. The day he was in Tehran, the most important crack down on reforms took place.

French interests are now in distancing itself from the regime.

After that I gave him details on the opposing forces in Iran, mainly religious Ayatollahs, who throughout Iran oppose the regime (you have the list), he wrote down the names.

When he noticed my hand written notes he said, "You are doing real intelligence work." My answer was that I am a political activist. Political activity without intelligence would be non-sense. He agreed.

At this stage he asked me if I send my information to Washington. My answer was, "Be sure. I send my information to anybody that could harm the regime!"

Then we discussed Iraq.

First, I explained to him why Ghom has no chance in winning the fight against Najaf. This is more evidence that the United States is aware of Iran's subversion.

Second, I said to him, I was in Tehran when the revolution happened. The political leadership was removed, but the country started to work after 1 month. The administration and the state structure was there to take care of the country. I gave him the example of Iran's national oil company. The board was changed, but the thousand employees continued their work. The same applies to events in Iraq. Within a month many things would be normal.

Before finishing the meeting we discussed at length the decision of Khameni to kill Arafat and its implications for the region.

We agreed to be in contact.

I am now almost sure that Tehran is planning another 11 September terrorist attack in the United States. We have mobilized everything to find more information. As soon as I have something more concrete, I will let you know, and under what conditions we can get details of this project.

Best regards,
Ali
May 3, 2003

Dear Curt,

Iran's opposition leaders had called today for a national strike. It has been the biggest referendum against the regime. The 2,200,000 teachers throughout Iran followed the strike call. Believe me everything is ready to get rid of the mafia terrorist regime. We have to move.

In my report I had mentioned the teachers as one of the main opposition forces.

Best regards,
Ali
May 3, 2003

Dear Curt,

In our report of April 21st, it was mentioned that Khamnei had issued orders Iran would take the initiative in targeting Americans everywhere; "preemptive terrorism." On Friday May 2, during the Friday prayer, Ayatollah Djanati, *head of the Council of Guardians*, made the decision of Khameni officially public, asking to attack without delay and without limitations, everywhere American interests.

Orders have been issued to all involved groups and forces. This is very serious.

Best regards,
Ali
May 4, 2003

Only for your eyes — Top secret.

Dear Curt,

Following the general strike of the teachers, the National Security Council had a meeting on the order of Khameni. Hassan Rouhani, the General Secretary of the National Security Council, has issued an order to all security and intelligence forces that any teacher demonstrating or not coming to his work or protesting should be arrested and punished. The extent and organized nature of the strike was completely unexpected for the regime.

Best regards,
Ali
Paris May 4, 2003

Urgent
Only for your eyes

Dear Curt,

First my sincere condolences for those innocent Americans killed today in Saudi Arabia by these criminals. I am coming back again to you, because it is my hope that my information may in some cases prevent such acts.

In my previous report I had mentioned that on the order of Khameni, in order to attack American and Israeli targets, a unified organization of terrorism under the leadership of Khameni has been created. This super-terror organization includes Hezballah, Hamas, Jihad Islamic, Ansar Hezballah, Sepah Badar, Al-Qaeda and the foreign legions of Sepah.

My information concerning the terrorist attack of today in Saudi Arabia has to be investigated in this context If the investigation about the killing of Americans in Saudi Arabia at Khobar Towers had not been blocked, to allow a deal between Iran and Saudi Arabia, the investigation would have been easier! The explosives from the recent attack have come from Dubai and the attack was carried out by Hezballah of Saudi Arabia. Saudi Arabia has been chosen, because Tehran assumes—as it has good relations with Saudi Arabia—people would not think of Iran's involvement.

In my fax of April 27, 2003, I had mentioned that Bagher Hakim will return to Iraq. It happened even sooner than we thought.

I have no contact with the State Department, so my information on the recent contacts between Tehran and USA and indirectly discussions with Hakim come from Tehran. Concerning the various discussions between Iran—USA, everybody shall have the opportunity to evaluate very quickly the lies of Tehran.

Concerning Hakim, our source tells us, he has promised to be a "good boy." The extremists are laughing at the naivete of the Americans! Your services should be able to identify very easily some of the terrorists and Guardian of Revolution from Iran who have come to Iraq as his entourage! He is asking to start, to have the Sharia laws! Independent of the fight between Ghom and Najaf for the Shiite power center, the Khameni example shows that naivete and compromise and wishful thinking can bring only catastrophe.

Concerning the importance of the trip of Khatami to Lebanon and Syria, it should be evaluated in the context that even his ceremonial role is being challenged by the extremists in Tehran and his power has been reduced to zero.

A few days ago his proposed law to increase his power was rejected and more and more of his supporters are being condemned and jailed. Khatami's entourage during his trip is revealing. It includes Mohtashami Poup, the godfather of Hezballah in Syria and former Foreign Minister Velyati, an extremist and advisor to Khameni.

Khameni in a defiant mood repeated again yesterday there cannot be any contact by Iran with the United States. In reaction the U.S. State Department said this message means we [Iranian counter-revolutionaries] should surrender and leave the scene. We shall never do that and we shall fight!

Dear Curt, whatever our cooperation, be sure that any time I have information that may save American lives, I shall not hesitate to make it available to you.

Best regards,
Ali
May 13, 2003

Dear Curt,

In spite of the fact that some people have raised questions about my sources, find please enclosed, some information. Next time I see you I shall give you my sources, so that you can judge yourself what risks and responsibility they are taking.

Whereas the Ministry of Intelligence has lost most of its power, the intelligence unit reporting directly to Khameni has become the real power and deciding center. Headed by Hejasi, well known terrorist, who worked with Fallahian at the Ministry of Intelligence. Other main members are Rezai of the intelligence of Sepah, *Parvig*, General with 2 stars, in charge of the personal security of the leader. Shemrani is deputy to Miphejasi. A commando of well trained officers from Sepah and the army is under the direct command of this intelligence unit. Their number is 1,000 and are located at Lavisan. They are in charge of any security issue brought up by the intelligence unit that has to be handled secretly. For instance, they are in charge of Bin Laden and other high ranking terrorists.

This intelligence unit is in continuous contact with Al-Qaeda and actions are coordinated. Al-Qaeda has been told it can always count on the support in any form from Iran, but it is also free to act independently. Bin Laden has again expressed his full support for Khameni as the leader of the Islamic world.

In two new training camps for terrorists created recently in the region south of Shiraz (Mamassani) there are 120 terrorists undergoing training. They are Arabs from Morocco, Tunisia, Algeria, Yemen, Libya. They all have European passports.

Concerning the terrorist attack against President George Bush, Sr., please note this follow up: two channels have been envisaged.

a) *Iranian businessman Los Angeles with Mexican connection.*

   On the order of Khameni the Iranian businessman channel was dropped because Khameni did not want a direct Iranian involvement.

b) *One of their companies in Dubai*, with business connections in the United States has been instructed to study the implementation of the terrorist project. This company has already been involved in terrorist activities. This is the second terrorist project against an American President. The first one was against President Reagan.

During a long session in Karaj (near Tehran) of the security and intelligence unit the terrorist project against United States has been discussed and decided. It forms 3 phases:

Phase I   Covers what we have just seen in Saudi Arabia and Morocco shall continue.

Phase II   Will strike at targets in Europe and shall start in August–September

Phase III   Concerns terrorist actions in the United States:

- An attack against a nuclear reactor by a plane to be hijacked in Canada. The name of the nuclear reactor mentioned but not clear begins with the letters "SEA..." (Seattle?) We will find out more information on the location. [Subsequently identified as the Seabrook Nuclear Reactor near Boston.]

- An attack with boat and explosives against the Statue of Liberty

- Boats and explosives against bridges

In the case of Saudi Arabia, Dubai and Jordan were used. In the terrorist attacks women play an increasing role. They travel easily to Tehran and back.

A report submitted to Khameni by Alahyori, who is an extremist professor at the university, has strongly recommended actions against the United States in Afghanistan and Iraq to prevent security and stability.

He has also argued that the United States has certainly found arms of mass destruction. Khameni has also the same opinion. Khameni believes the United States will give the information out when it is politically the best moment.

Concerning Iraq:

a) Agents have informed Iran that a terrorist project against the United States is being prepared at Al Divamie. (These agents are in Moussel in Iraq.)

b) Explosions are being provided to terror units in Baghdad to prevent security and repair of services.

A report from Iran's Foreign Ministry expert says, as M6 has no sympathy with Israel, M6 reports are more favorable to Iran. However, Britain's Defense Minister is the worst enemy!

Tehran hopes that it may succeed to bring about a defense agreement with France and some countries of the region in Europe. (They are dreaming!)

Contacts and discussions are continuing with North Korea.

Best regards
Ali
May 17, 2003

Dear Curt,

Top Secret

In Varamin (near Tehran) in Parshin a top secret center is working. All doctors, engineers and high level technical working people who have access to the site, have to go through intelligence training; how they have to behave, even within their families— so that the secrecy of their activity is kept. Their eyes are covered when they are taken to the site. A total of 500 high level technical people are working there. This center is cooperating with the center in [illegible].

Our source is telling us this site is involved in producing chemical and biological products. However a connection with Iran's atomic program cannot be ruled out, in our opinion.

Concerning the facilities of Iran's atomic program in Natanz, should the inspectors go there, they should not limit themselves to the facilities on the surface. A "James Bond town" is deep below.

In 1988, students from Saudi Arabia were studying in the United States. They went back to Iran. Their Sheikh and leader was Al Sadre. They have had contact with Al-Qaeda and Iraq. They called themselves the "Soldiers of God." For years they kept quiet due to the good relations of Iran–Saudi Arabia. But due to their cooperation with Al-Qaeda they have been involved in the bombing in Saudi Arabia.

Dear Curt, as long as the terrorist generator, Iran, has not been silenced, this is to continue.

Best regards,
Ali
May 18, 2003

5

ALI REPORTS

12–22 June 2003

"Rafsanjani told [Muqtada al Sadr] that with Iran's support the possibilities in Iraq are much more important in
Iraq than what the Hezballah has done in Lebanon. There
would be no limit to Iran's assistance and cooperation."

—Ali

By June, the honeymoon was over in Iraq for U.S. and allied forces. But the full-scale terrorist onslaught against Iraq's liberators had not yet begun. On June 10, a *Washington Post* headline reported, "U.S. Soldiers Face Growing Resistance; Attacks in Central Iraq More Frequent and Sophisticated."

Events were unfolding just as Ali warned that they would. Highlights of Ali's June reports:

- Accurately anticipates the rise of Ayatollah Muqtada al Sadr as a leader of anti-U.S. violence in Iraq.

- Notes that the Secret Service was concerned about the plot to assassinate former president George H. W. Bush. CIA still showed no interest in his information.

- Describes the failed dissident uprising in Iran that Ali had accurately forecast (almost to the day) in earlier reports. He emphasizes that the uprising was not sponsored by the counter-revolutionary organization, which remains intact.

June 12, 2003
Confidential—Only for your eyes—Urgent

Dear Curt,

As expected, demonstrations took place again last night in Tehran. I believe this information that I am sending you herewith is very important for developments in Iraq and Middle East.

A) Ayatollah Seyed Mohammed Sadre was the leader of Iraqi Shiite. He was an Iraqi Shiite. His Iraqi origin could be traced back hundreds of years. The other Ayatollah was one of Iranian origin. He was murdered in 1999 by Saddam's henchmen and presented as an alternative by Iranian Shiite to get rid of this Iraqi Shiite. His son Hijat al Islam Moghtada Sadre, has been also known for his opposition to the regimes that killed his father. (His associates have been blamed for killing recently Sheikh Khoie.) The young Sadre being of Iraqi origin has not been associated with Iran and has not been exposed in this respect.

Tehran has decided to take advantage of young Sadre's origin and situation for its goals and policies in Iraq.

He was invited to Iran and after many discussions he had lunch on June 8 with Rafsanjani. Rafsanjani told him, Iran would give him unlimited support so that he becomes, like Hassan Nassrollah in Lebanon, the key figure of the Shiite movement in Lebanon and in charge of Hezballah of Iraq which could become, and is being developed as, the most important organization in Iraq.

Rafsanjani told him that with (Moghtada Sadre) Iran's support the possibilities in Iraq are much more important in Iraq than what Hezballah has done in Lebanon. There would be no limit to Iran's assistance and cooperation.

Full agreement was reached between Rafsanjani and the young Sadre. Like Hezballah in Lebanon, who obliged Israel to leave South Lebanon, Hezballah in Iraq would destabilize the United States in Iraq and oppose American occupation of Iraq. Tehran has decided that everything should be done to prevent the United States from achieving its goals in Iraq.

B) During the last visit of President Assad to Tehran a few weeks ago, Tehran succeeded in persuading Assad that they should fully cooperate and that Iran–Syria and Lebanon should stand up against the United States. The argument brought up by Tehran is that the smallest concession to the United States would be interpreted by U.S. as weakness and encourage America to widen its demands. "One inch retreat would mean a demand of 10 meters!" In this context it was agreed that Iraqi human assets—gold—cash—"equipment" in control and at the disposal of Syria will not be handed over to the United States.

C) After the meeting at Sharm el Sheikh at Aqaba, Khameni has ordered his terrorist network that by all means the execution of the United States road map has to be prevented and destroyed!

D) After the meeting in Aqaba, Mohtashami, the godfather of Hezballah in Lebanon, went to Beirut to discuss the situation with Hezballah. In a meeting with the central committee of Hezballah he declared the minimum we shall do is "to throw all the Israelis into the sea!"

Best regards,
Ali
June 12, 2003

Dear Curt,

I had the meeting with a U.S. Government agent. It was not the CIA contact that we hoped for, to investigate all the issues raised in my faxes to you. It was a special agent of the Department of the Treasury, US Secret Service, limited to subject of the information concerning the plot to assassinate President George Bush, Senior.

Best regards,
Ali
June 22, 2003

Dear Curt,

Below find my analysis of the real center of power in Teheran and of the basic policies of that power center:

Power center: Khameni—Rafsanjani—Hejazi (Hassan)

BASIC POLICIES:

A) Internal Policies: Crushing of any opposition and dissent. The will of the Iranian elite comes first.

B) Foreign Policy: Attacking and destabilizing United States presence in Afghanistan, Iraq, countries around Caspian Sea, (former countries of Soviet Union), Lebanon.

C) Gaining Time: Tehran believes that from January 2004, the United States shall be involved in elections and could not get involved in any move abroad. In the coming months Tehran shall "play around" and try to mislead the United States and Europe.

	For instance, last Tuesday it was decided by Khameni, if in the case international pressure for inspection of its atomic bomb program becomes very strong, Iran would sign the protocol, but would in fact find all kinds of excuses to postpone the inspections.
D) Speed Up:	Activities and efforts to have the atom bomb enabling Iran to achieve a strategic advantage like North Korea.

Best regards,
Ali
June 22, 2003

Dear Curt,

The decision taken by Khameni at the start of the demonstration was confirmed Thursday at a meeting headed by Khameni that the demonstrations shall be crushed and suppressed by all means available!

My evaluation is that the "Mullah Mafia" will be able to achieve its goal: The demonstration lacks the necessary organization and coordination and the various means required for a successful uprising. The movement is facing hardliners who are by no means ready to give in.

Furthermore, for the above reasons, the "safety net" and its whole organization, able to bring about change, as I discussed with you in Paris *are not involved*. Consequently, the organization is intact and was not destroyed when Khameni crushed the demonstrators. As of Sunday evening 3,716 people were arrested.

The number covers arrests by Sepah and official security forces. To this figure should be added those arrested by the Intelligence Ministry and the Judiciary. The figure of arrested demonstrators could be as high as 6,000. There are 611 wounded and 11 killed. I shall keep you informed on the coming events.

Best regards,
Ali
June 22, 2003

6

ALI REPORTS

July–August 2003

"Al Qaeda has gotten a green light for a terrorist attack on
the United States bigger than 9/11."

—*Ali*

THE 12TH IMAM OPERATION, a terrorist attack worse than the September 11 attacks, is mentioned for the first time in Ali's report of August 25, 2003. The attack is originally scheduled for the twelfth imam's birthday, during the period November 25–26. However, in a later report, the Committee of Nine decides to delay the attack until after the 2004 U.S. presidential elections.

Tehran was concerned that another terrorist attack directly on the United States might rally the American people behind President Bush, ensuring his reelection. The Committee of Nine prefers "anyone but Bush" as U.S. president. Iraq becomes the battlefield where they hope to break the will of the United States and defeat President Bush's bid for reelection.

Ali notes that the failed plan to attack the Seabrook Nuclear Reactor is not the 12th Imam operation. Another, unknown, attack is planned. However, Ali told us that the 12th Imam operation could include another attempt to attack Seabrook or some other nuclear reactor.

Dear Curt,

Following your recommendations, I was contacted by the CIA yesterday. We had a meeting of about 2 hours at lunch. It was more about generalities, still no real action toward working with my people, and no real interest in a working arrangement to get information from my sources. I was told they would contact me again in a few days.

Thanks and Best Regards,
Ali
July 2, 2003

Dear Curt,

Thank you for your telephone call. As I told you the two Iranians you met in London are close to the Mafia in Tehran. They put up good faces to mislead everybody. To substantiate my claim, please find below some information on their background:

1) Djavaid Mansauri. Before the Iranian revolution he was a member of the Islamic National Party. He was very close to Ayatollah Beheschti and Ayatollah Ardebili.

   He created after the revolution the Sepah (Guardian of Revolution) and was the first head of Sepah! After the purge at the Foreign Ministry, he went to the Foreign Ministry, became Ambassador to Pakistan. As an Islamic extremist, he was responsible for the fights between Shiites and Sunnis in Pakistan. His best job was head of the Consulate at the Foreign Ministry to teach the "diplomats" on their abilities abroad. As deputy of the Foreign Minister he reports directly and only to Khameni.

2) Khazempour Ardebili. He is in charge of purchases of NIOL, (National Oil Company). His career is the Ministry of Oil. He was at OPEC.

He is close to Rafsanjani and reports only to him. (He is involved in the corrpution of the Rafsanjani family.

Our source tells us:

1) Besides the attack on atomic facilities in Seattle [inferred from the target having the letters "Sea..."]—we mentioned to you—they are also studying the possibility of an attack [on an atomic plant] in the Boston area.

2) Tehran believes it will be an atomic power within 50 days.

Yesterday Iran has decided to close all Iraqi offices belonging to the opposition to Saddam Hussein and send everybody back to Iraq. The reason for this decision is to pretend there are no Iraqis in Iran who could interfere in Iraq.

Best regards,
Ali
July 18, 2003

Confidential—Top secret—Only for your eyes

Dear Curt,

I send you enclosed some information, even if it is only for the record. I am sure with your help we will win the fight!

Around 15–20 days ago the high ranking extremists had a meeting with Khameni. He declared, "Today is an historic day which will go down as the most important day in Iran's history." We believe this special meeting was called with regard to Iran's successful atomic bomb program.

A report was submitted to Khameni from his intelligence unit coordinating with Al Qaeda. The report stated, "The terrorist attack of 9/11 was originally planned for July. Due to a problem with one of the pilots, it was delayed."

Before Iraq war, Khameni had received a report from his intelligence service in which the doctrine of the Bush administration was analyzed. It was explained that the United States plans regime change in Afghanistan, Iraq, Syria and Iran.

In a discussion of this report after the U.S. invasion of Iraq, the Council of Nine decided, should Syria be attacked, then there is no doubt Iran would be the next target.

Consequently, if Syria is attacked, the Council of Nine has decided that Iran would not wait, but act preemptively. For this purpose, 50 terrorist attacks abroad have been prepared.

It has been agreed by all terrorist organizations, all terrorist actions shall be carried out in the name of Hezballah.

The Al-Qaeda camp in Chazvin has been moved to the heights of the mountain of Damavand. Security forces are keeping the camp. (With your satellite, you can observe the camp.)

Bin Laden has left his place in Tehran. We do not yet know where he is relocated.. We are trying to find out.

Before September 15, there will be a message from Bin Laden.

From Iran's coordination committee, Al Qaeda has got a green light for a terrorist attack on the United States, bigger than 9/11. The date is about 25–26 November. The attack is deliberately timed to coincide with the anniversary of the 12th

Imam, a most frightening sign. In Shiite Islamic theology, the 12th Imam, called the Mahdi, is a Messianic figure whose return to Earth will bring the justice of God, and the destruction of all infidels. The 12th Imam is like your Christian Apocalypse. Iran's Council of Nine sees the next big terrorist attack on the United States as being like this. The attack they are planning will be like the return of the 12th Imam.

Terrorist attacks are also planned on foreigners in Iraq in order to mobilize public opinion against the United States.

Sepah believes U.S. coalition forces will find arms of mass destruction in Iraq. Sepah has learned from Iraqis that some of these arms have been moved to Syria. Some weapons of mass destruction are hidden deep under earth, close to a small airport.

As the number of American helicopters have increased at the Iran–Iraq border, Iranian missiles have been moved to the area.

We informed you in our previous reports that three high ranking Iraqis had fled to Iran. Through their contacts in Iraq, they are trying to arrange the coming of Saddam Hussein to Iran. Iran has agreed. They hope to succeed in the next 60 days. (We may have a summit of Khameni, Bin Laden, Saddam Hussein, Mullah Omar Hakmatyar!)

Terrorist attacks are planned against opposition personalities abroad. Eight people have been targeted in the United States. The attacks are expected to start from January–February 2004.

Best regards,
Ali
August 25, 2003

Dear Curt:

I sent the below to CIA.

Attention CIA, Washington

Your representative called me yesterday. You are certainly aware of our discussions. He said he would call me again on Friday. Your agent did not mention the arrests of terrorists in Canada. It is obvious that you have benefitted from the information on this terrorist operation that I gave you in 3 faxes through Congressman Curt Weldon:

1) "An attack against an atomic plant by a plane, the name mentioned, but not clear is begins with "Sea..." [Seattle?] We will find out more information on the location." Afterward we found out that the idea was to fly in a plane from Canada to attack the Seabrook nuclear reactor.

2) "Besides the attack on atomic facilities, we mentioned to you, they are also studying the possibility of an attack in the Boston area."

3) "We have brought up again the terrorist attack against an atomic plant. When we asked how with the existing security arrangements, even concerning the cockpit such a thing could be done the answer was: *It is no problem to fly into the United States from neighboring countries!*"

I hope these arrests may prevent their planning for a terrorist attack on the United States worse than September 11.

Best regards,
Ali
August 27, 2003

7

ALI REPORTS

4–27 September 2003

"The big powers have kept the atomic bomb technology as
the most important secret and are preventing others from
obtaining the technology. But young, able Iranians have
succeeded in their work to achieve this technology."

—*Ayatollah Khameni*

THE SEPTEMBER ALI REPORTS IDENTIFY secret sites where Iran is developing nuclear weapons, with the assistance of foreign scientists from
North Korea, China, and Russia. The report of September 27, 2003,
describes Iran as pursuing a policy of deliberate deception, cheating
on its anti-nuclear agreement with European powers to secretly pursue the A-bomb. This intelligence may be of interest to Britain, Germany, and France, who have recently (November 2004) extracted
another pledge from Iran to respect the nuclear Non-Proliferation
Treaty. Other highlights:

- Iran hosts terrorist mastermind and butcher Abu Musab al Zarqawi.

- Iran escalates the terrorist war against the United States in Iraq.

- At a secret meeting of the Committee of Nine, Ayatollah Khameni
  declares, "The twelfth imam, on the birthday of the Madhi, we shall
  witness the destruction of the United States."

Dear Curt:

Back in Washington you have certainly seen my latest fax, in which there is some important information, most of all on the terrorist attack planned for November, the "12th Imam." Please find enclosed some new information.

1) Bin Laden has left Tehran. We have no information where he is. We believe there is a probability of 50% that he has left Iran.

2) Terrorist mastermind Dr. Alzavaheri and Mognie and 25 other arabs took part at a dinner in a villa north of Karaj. After the dinner, they were moved to "Manjil region" protected by special forces.

3) At Iran's Foreign Ministry, at the desk on the United States, a total of 160 people are working. They have all modern technological facilities at their disposal. A certain number of them are engaged in getting information on all American personalities, politicians, journalists, etc. Their private lives, preferences, weaknesses, etc. Three Americans are cooperating with them. Two of them have become religious and are in Ghom. All United States and British newspapers are analyzed and a report submitted to the Council of Nine under Khameni.

4) Since the collapse of the regime in Iraq, 90,000 Iranians have gone back to Iraq. Among them there are forces organized into three "Army Corps" (1,000 agents in each corp). They are pasdaran, from the intelligence. Their agents speak Arabic, and some of them are Afghans. They are with special mobile terror units and receive orders from Tehran. This program is to prepare a large range of terrorist actions against the coalition forces starting in January–February when elections start in the United States.

5) In a meeting under Khameni with high ranking members of the Sepah and Army, all the plans to counter any American attack were discussed. Costs of several billion dollars were approved if required.

6) In the following a summary of statements by Khameni:

a) "There are threats of military action against us. But Iran is different from Iraq. After their mismanagement in Iraq, the United States is unable to act militarily against us. But in any case we are ready. Let them think they can act by sponsoring a popular uprising in Iran. They do not understand our country. There is no difference between Shiite and Sunni. Our coordination is working. The 12th Imam, on the birthday of the Mahdi [November 23–25], we shall witness the destruction of the United States."

b) "These days some people are coming to see me. They are worried about the threat from the United States, about the future of Iran. I tell them they should not worry because we have made all the necessary arrangements to triumph over the United States. In any case, even if I am wrong, we are all martyrs for Islam.

c) Concerning relations with the United States, there is no need for intermediaries. "If the United States accepts all our previous conditions, if the United States now accepts not to intervene in our internal affairs, and if the United States leaves Iraq, so that it becomes an Islamic Republic, I shall then speak to the United States!"

Best regards,
Ali
September 4, 2003

Dear Curt,

In our fax of August 25 we wrote:

Around 15–20 days ago the high ranking extremists had a meeting with Khameni. Khameni declared, "Today is a historic day, which will go down as the most important day in Iran's history." We believe this special meeting was called with regard to Iran's successful atomic bomb program.

Today Khameni has declared:

"The big powers have kept the atomic bomb technology as the most important secret and are preventing others from obtaining the technology. But young, able Iranians have succeeded in their work to achieve this technology. The reaction of the arrogant United States is the current campaign against us." Khameni did not mention all the experts from Russia, the former Soviet Union, China, and North Korea, who are all in Iran!

Since the agreement reached with the European Foreign Ministers to reassure them that Iran does not seek nuclear weapons, production of enriched uranium for atomic bombs has increased by about 80%.

Sites at which the regime is trying to hide its atomic bomb activities, include:

a) The mountains of Hamedan

b) Semnan

c) Isphahan (This is an ideal site for the international inspections, since Iran probably cannot remove or hide the facility located there!)

US–Iranian relations:

Recent weak statements by United States officials (Mr. Armitage, etc.) are being interpreted that Tehran's defiance has obliged the Bush administration to retreat from its hard stand on "no A-bomb for Iran." The U.S. Secretary of State is considered in Tehran as the best friend of Tehran. Colin Powell is much more appreciated than even former President Clinton and his Secretary of State!

The agreement with Europe has reduced pressure on Iran and Iran has succeeded in buying time to continue its atomic bomb program. Consequently, Iran has decided in order to be fully successful and oblige the United States to forgo any action against Iran, maximum pressure has to be put on the United States in Afghanistan, Iraq, and Pakistan.

a) Concerning Iraq, we have already mentioned to you large scale crossing from Iran into Iraq of terrorists. Large scale subversion will start in January or December.

b) 20,000 Afghani have been trained by Iran. Under the cover of, "Return of Afghani to their country," terrorists are sent into Afghanistan for subversion.

c) With large financial help from Iran, extremists have been mobilized to destabilize the Iraq and Afghanistan.

Last Sunday, an official Iranian government car was bombed. The car was supposed to take the Ayatollah Nouri to Khameni. But he was not in the car.

The list of 200 so called Al Qaeda members "given to the United Nations" are drug people from various countries arrested by Iran on the drug business on the Iranian borders.

Best regards,
Ali
September 27, 2003

8

ALI REPORTS

11–30 October 2003

"The code for the operation is 'Ya Mahdi, Ad Rekni!'"

—*Ali*

THE REPORT OF OCTOBER 30, 2003, is of particular interest, as it provides some details about the 12th Imam operation, code named "Ya Mahdi, Ad Rekni!" This translates as an appeal to the twelfth imam by his familiar name: "Mahdi, Save Us!"

The 12th Imam operation involves another attempt to attack a U.S. nuclear reactor with an airliner hijacked in Canada. The report notes that the Committee of Nine is still divided about whether to proceed with the attack or to wait until after the 2004 presidential election.

Other highlights:

- Details on Iran's cheating on international agreements to develop atomic weapons illegally.

- Details on the assassination plot against the elder President Bush.

- Details on Iran's terrorist war in Iraq.

Dear Curt:

Please find enclosed information from my source.

Atomic Bomb

A) A committee set up to decide on Iran's policy concerning the signing of the protocol has decided:

   a) It is Khameni who should take the final decision

   b) Rafsanjani made public Iran's conditions for any inspection. The experts would have no right to visit religious locations, (Ghom, Meshed) military strategic locations that would endanger the security of the country, strategic oil facilities.

   c) These limitations are connected to the order of Khameni of September 15, asking that all atomic facilities and equipment to be removed until October 5, from the 3 (three) known locations and hidden in 7 (seven). These places are those which Rafsanjani has declared the experts have no right to visit.

Khameni's reaction to the report of the committee has been:

   a) The experts can visit only the three known locations

   b) Our atomic capacities are more important than North Korea. There are several other atomic locations unknown to the International Atomic Energy Agency.

   c) North Korea knows our capacities and is more close to us than any Islamic country.

   d) We have no reason to sign the additional protocol.

B) *Terrorist project against President George Bush Senior:*

The project has been discussed with a Kashmiri Muslim in Dubai, who has an exchange office there. He had accepted to carry out the project against the payment of $5 million, with the help of the Mexican mafia. The project discussed was to kill the former president at the opening ceremony of a theater. We don't know if the project has been given up or not. We are trying to find out.

C) A special committee for study and evaluation of foreign policy connected to Iranian intelligence has submitted a report to Khameni. Main points of the report are:

If up to now it was agreed that Al Queda was free to act in line with its own decisions; in the future, any action in the United States should be fully coordinated with Tehran. The reason being that any big action by Al Queda in USA would mobilize behind President Bush the population and ensure his re-election, whereas today the President is in big trouble.

Consequently, the best policy against the USA is guerilla warfare in Afghanistan and Iraq, to kill as many as possible American soldiers and destabilize these countries. This is the best way to prevent his re-election and gives us the possibility to influence the American election. We will know next week the reaction and decision of Khameni.

D) Tehran believes that from December the United States shall face in Afghanistan attacks from concentrated and orderly regrouped Taliban forces.

E) Sepah has informed Khameni that with the organization in place they can move to try to create problems and destabilize the situation in Pakistan.

Best regards,

Ali

October 11, 2003

Dear Curt:

Find enclosed the fax you asked me. I know you have been doing anything possible to solve the financial problem. I have also done what I can to keep the source. We have done both what we were able. Now if the administration does not want human intelligence, OK. Good luck to them.

Best regards,

Ali

October 30, 2003

Dear Curt:

Around 6 months ago in a meeting with Rafsanjani, Khameni brought up the issue of payments made by foreign companies to persons very close to the regime. Such payments should be stopped to prevent the enemies of the regime to spread accusations and rumors. Khameni argued there are $6–7 million in foreign banks with our signature. From these bank accounts we can make any payments required. Both agreed to stop payments of commissions to well known persons of the regime.

When a few weeks ago the payments made to the son of Rafsanjani in Oslo were revealed, Khameni was very upset. The payment was confirmed to him by a special envoy sent to Oslo and he had a very harsh reaction.

On the order of Khameni, a special committee of ten members was created:

a) Nategh Nouri

b) Velayati (former Foreign Minister)

c) The brother of Larijani

d) Hassan Ruheni

e) Hejasi

f) Reza Shahri

g) Khameni's special advisor to the Foreign Ministry

h) 3 Bazaris very close to the regime

All these members have their own dedicated followers. Issues discussed by Khameni in the meeting of the above committee:

a) This committee shall meet twice a week to report any important event with special focus on cases of corruption.

b) It is wrong-doings similar to what the son of Rafsanjani has done which are the biggest danger for the regime. There is no danger from abroad. The Americans cannot do anything. We know they haven't given any financial help to the opposition. They think they can change the regime from within Iran. They believe in this stupid possibility and it is in our interest to let them have this idiotic illusion.

c) If something happens to me you are responsible for the safeguard of the regime.

d) Hassan Rouhani, (his real name is Feridum Rouhani) has all the required qualities to be the next President. (Velayati didn't appreciate)

The decisions taken by Khameni have resulted in a power struggle between Khameni and Rafsanjani. Several facts are self telling:

a) The committee is to be put in charge if something happens to Khameni.

b) It is well known that during all these years any important foreign delegations going to Tehran have had a meeting with Rafsanjani. When the three European Foreign Ministers arrived in Tehran, Rafsanjani had gone to Shiraz. Furthermore, on Friday in the prayer, he did not say a word about the above issue. He knows that there is no possibility of a solution. He is preparing himself to use the issue against Khameni, who has got himself "involved."

There should be no misunderstanding: The "soi disant" involvement of Khameni is only intended to mislead the Europeans to think that Iran is serious about negotiating away Iran's A-bomb program!

The real position of Khameni is shown in a letter by seventeen high ranking Sepah members:

"We know you are opposed to an agreement. On your orders, we have moved and hidden all the atomic equipment. We are sure you will not retreat from making Iran's Islamic A-bomb."

c) In the committee set up to discuss Iran's atomic policy two proposals were discussed: One rejection of the protocol intended to stop Iran's A-bomb. The second, signing the protocol, play the game and buy time to execute the program. Our source tells us after the visit of the Foreign Ministers, some issues were still open. Limitations of locations to be visited and enrichment of uranium. The quantity of enriched uranium has increased by 21% until today (October 29).

Iran's limitations on inspection rights of the UN's International Atomic Energy Agency covers strategic, military, religious sites and the whole complex of Khameni. A main problem for Tehran is the story of enriched uranium we mentioned to you when you were in Paris. Another play to buy time is Tehran's insistence that the European countries have to guarantee officially transfer of atomic know how to Iran.

In a report submitted by Khameni's committee of experts, it is argued Europe will permit Iran to get away with anything, especially if European economic interests can profit. United States policies will not be followed and approved by Europe. There are $32 billion in signed agreements (mainly French and British) which are expandable to about $50 billion.

With regard to the meeting with the three European Foreign Ministers, Tehran is very satisfied with the British and the French, but the German Foreign Minister is criticized.

We had mentioned to you that Iran is planning an experimental atomic explosion around October 18. The postponement has no technical reason, but it has been a political decision. Following the "agreement" with the European Foreign Ministers, Tehran believes it has succeeded in buying time to continue with its program secretly. A blast at this stage would jeopardize everything. The next step will depend on the report of the UN Atomic Agency.

d) In our previous reports we mentioned an attack of Al-Qaeda in the United States November 25–26. Our source gives us the following information:

1) The attack is planned November 25–December 3

2) Location, U.S. atomic installations near the Canadian border are targeted.

3) Means, plane, to be hijacked in Canada.

4) The code for the operation is "Ya Mahdi, Ad Rekni!"

5) In the plan, drugs will be used, so that everybody becomes unconscious on the airliner so there can be no interference from passengers with the execution of the operation.

6) Final decision will not be taken in the coordination committee with Al Qaeda, but by the Committee of Nine. We shall inform you on the final decision on November 9. We told you in our last fax that some experts have been arguing that an attack at this stage could mobilize people behind President Bush.

During Ramadan two important "eftar" (religious dinners) are planned in Tehran with Khameni. The dinners will be held on the 4th day of Ramadan and 19th day of Ramadan. On the 4th, participants are the terrorist Emad Mognie with his team of five. On the 19th , master terrorist Alzavaheri with his team of five. Presence of Bin Laden is not forseen.

Tehran believes its border with Iraq cannot be controlled by the coalition forces. Many Iraqis of the old regime are in Iran, among them 33 of the special forces of Saddam Hussein. Sepah is in charge to organize these forces for subversion in Iraq. We believe it is useful to watch the area of Dehloran on the Iran–Iraq border.

Tehran is decided to destabilize by all means Iraq, because it is persuaded that a stable, free, democratic, Iraq is the worst poison for the Islamic republic. Tehran has a similar approach to Afghanistan. Under the cover that the Afghanis living in Iran must return to Afghanistan, a force of 20,000 has been trained by Sepah and is being sent back to Afghanistan for subversion. Concentrated attacks will start from December.

Tehran is supporting Saudi Arabia, whereas Iran thinks Abdallah of Jordan cannot be trusted. Concerning Basra, Tehran is not satisfied because the British are rather successful in controlling the area.

Tehran is building its desk for Egypt. 300 people have been mobilized and the brother of the killer of Anwar Sadat is in charge of them. Tehran has come to the conclusion Egypt could face an Islamic take over and wants to have in place "Hezballah organization," similar to Lebanon.

Iraq has moved its arms of mass destruction to Syria and Iran. Forty percent are in Iran. Sixty percent have gone from Syria to Lebanon and are kept by Hezballah deep in the mountains.

Air force: Iran has succeeded in obtaining advanced radars and spare parts for its Phantoms and helicopters.

The "Fedayeen of Khameni," 4,000–5,000 strong are trained in Ali Abad Ghom. They will act as urban guerilla forces should the United States attack Iran.

Best regards,
Ali
October 30, 2003

9

ALI REPORTS

19 November 2003

"If Iran is submitted for sanctions to the U.N. Security
Council, we are ready for martyrdom and will do everything to destroy our enemies."

—Ayatollah Khameni

IN NOVEMBER 2003, AT A CRUCIAL meeting of the Committee of Nine, it is decided to postpone the 12th Imam attack on the United States until after the 2004 presidential elections. From the minutes of the meeting, detailed reasons are provided for delaying "Ya Mahdi, Ad Rekni!"

Nonetheless, Ayatollah Khameni also decides that, "The project should be kept alive and preparations should be made in such a way that once the decision is taken to go ahead, there is no delay in execution."

November 19, 2003

Very confidential—Only For Your eyes

Dear Curt,

Find below please the latest developments concerning the project "Ya Mahdi, Ad Rekni!" I had told you previously Khameni is taking his decision on whether or not to proceed with this operation after November 9.

Iran's committee of political experts has recommended that the project should be postponed until after the American elections for the following reasons:

1) As one of Iran's principal goals is to prevent the re-election of President Bush, any attack would mobilize the American people behind the President, whereas actually the support for President Bush is diminishing regularly with regard to the situation in Iraq.

2) Any attack at that scale on American soil could result in a military action against Iran. American history shows an American president at war never loses an election.

3) Consequently, everything should be done to increase American difficulties in Afghanistan, Pakistan, Egypt and mainly in Iraq, where the more Americans are killed the less President Bush has a chance to be re-elected.

4) A free, democratic, Iraq is poison to the Islamic republic.

5) Furthermore, any stabilization of the situation in Iraq would free the United States to move against Iran.

In the meeting of the Council of Nine, Khameni has agreed with postponing the big terrorist attack on the United States, but has made the following qualifications and comments:

a) The project should be kept alive and preparations should be made in such a way that once the decision is taken to go ahead, there is no delay in the execution.

b) Khameni has instructed Sepah and other Iranian intelligence intensify the cooperation with Al Qaeda throughout the world, and especially in the United States preparing for attacks on U.S. targets.

c) Iran's policies and decisions shall be affected by its relations with the UN Atomic Agency. If there is no agreement amenable to Iran, we shall cancel even our pretense at cooperation and give the United states a lesson it will never forget.

Khameni can never accept that Israel has an atomic bomb whereas Iran is denied the right to have one.

According to Khameni, "In the region we are the strongest country. We have the best missiles. We can read the heart of Europe. For the experimental atomic blast we have succeeded in obtaining the 'product' (enriched uranium) and the 'starters' for igniting a nuclear explosion.

"If Iran is submitted for sanctions to the UN Security Council, we are ready for martyrdom and will do everything to destroy our enemies."

"In last resort we would not hesitate to blow up our nuclear plant in Bushehr to contaminate the whole area. We would create an oil crisis by letting our oil flow into the Persian Gulf and put it on fire and close the Strait of Hormuz."

In our last report, we reported the planned "eftar" (religious dinner) of Emad Mognie with Khameni. It has taken place and Mognie wasted no time to express his thanks for the terrorist explosion in Turkey!

Best regards,
Ali
November 19, 2003

10

ALI REPORTS

21–29 January 2004

"Everything should be done to ensure the victory of the
Democratic candidate in the United States Presidential
election of November."

—*Ayatollah Khameni*

IN NOVEMBER 2003, I PROVIDED the House Permanent Select Committee on Intelligence (HPSCI) and the Senate Select Committee on
Intelligence (SSCI) the full record of Ali's reports, up to that point. I
met personally with HPSCI members to warn them of a possible
impending terrorist attack. In my letter to HPSCI chairman Porter
Goss and SSCI chairman Pat Roberts, I wrote:

> *This letter is to warn you of an intelligence failure in the process of
> happening. My hope is that, by holding hearings or conducting an
> investigation, you can correct this ongoing failure in intelligence
> that, if left uncorrected, could result in a catastrophe for the United
> States greater than the terrorist attacks of September 11.*

To their credit, the House and Senate intelligence committees pressed
the intelligence community to work with Ali. This resulted in a hope-
ful Christmas season meeting between Ali and the CIA. But by January 2004, as Ali's report of January 21 indicates, the CIA was again
deaf and blind. The CIA's cooperation with Ali lasted only until other

matters distracted HPSCI and SSCI, and then it went back to "business as usual."

The January missives from Ali also:

- Explain why Tehran would prefer a Democrat to replace President Bush in the White House.

- Emphasize again that the war in Iraq is aimed at unseating President Bush.

- Warn that Iran has purchased missile and warhead technology from Pakistan.

Dear Curt,

As you have asked me to keep you always informed, may I mention below some developments:

1) My meeting with the representative of CIA in Paris before Christmas, which as I told you seemed to me positive, as he promised me he would contact me very soon. But I haven't had any further contact with him.

2) Even if the administration is not interested in any information from us (they probably have their own informants!), and although we have many problems with our sources because we have not been able to fulfill our financial promises, may I send you as a friend the following information, I got last night:

   a) In a meeting with his closest advisers Khameni has decided:

   - There should be no relations with the United States.

   - *Everything*, should be done to ensure the victory of the Democratic candidate in the United States presidential election of November.

     It was argued that a Democratic president would have a more positive position toward Tehran. Further because any new administration would need time to get installed and formulate its policies, this would give Tehran the needed time to push ahead with its designs, (most important in the field of atomic weapons).

   - In order to help defeat President Bush, Tehran believes that destabilizing Iraq and killing of Americans is the most important weapon at its disposal.

Dear Curt, as I told you before, expect from Iran anything you can imagine in Iraq against the U.S. coalition.

I have the feeling, the administration is aware of the developments and Iran's role, but wrongly thinks it can play around until after the presidential election in November.

3) It is also known, Iran has bought from Pakistan technology and drawings to build warheads for cruise missiles. For your information, three of them will be ready soon.

Best regards,
Ali
January 21, 2004

Dear Curt

I am sure your trip to Libya was most successful. I saw you on television. All my congratulations. I am sure also you may have got interesting information about Iran.

We have got some information on Iran–Pakistan cooperation in the atomic bomb field.

We are facing again the lies from Tehran. Did Tehran obtain, as pretended by the Mullahs, information to create an atomic plant to produce electricity? My source tells me, Tehran obtained the technology to produce atomic bombs and warheads! I have no doubt about my source. For your information the nuclear expert from Pakistan has got a villa at the Caspian sea.

Best regards,
Ali
January 29, 2004

11

ALI REPORTS

3–22 February 2004

"Concerning Tehran's atom bomb program, I can't hardly
  add anything. Everything is coming out as we discussed."

—Ali

THE QUOTE ABOVE REFERS TO REPORTS appearing in the Western press
about Iran's advanced A-bomb program. News reports confirmed
what Ali's sources had been telling us back in April 2003: Iran was
closer to developing nuclear weapons than suspected in the West. Ironically, according to some press reports, the advanced state of Iran's
nuclear weapons program took the U.S. intelligence community by
surprise.

Dear Curt:

Fortunately, it seems your intelligence organizations are following closely the danger of plans for attacks on targets in the United States, as we discussed before.

According to my sources one can expect other actions in the United States by sleeping Al-Qaeda units within USA. As soon as the financial problem is solved, we should be able to get more information.

There will be increasing efforts by the Al-Qaeda–Khameni Mafia to destabilize Iraq.

The American administration has created during the last two years a lot of good will with the Iranian people. This is jeopardized by all this talk about... American–Iranian dialogue, etc. I know all this does not mean anything serious. But the people of my country, like other countries in the region, are fixated on conspiracy theories. People are starting to think that the United States, like Europe, wants to keep the Mullahs in power. This is, for future relations between the United States and the coming new Iran, a tragedy.

Again, my thanks for your efforts and the confidence you have shown towards me.

Best regards,
Ali
February 3, 2004

Dear Curt:

1) Reference my last fax, concerning enriched uranium found in Iraq, I can only confirm.

2) What I regret is that when you were in Paris and we discussed the issue, you said "I am ready to go myself to Iraq and have a look at the place." Unfortunately some people instead of helping prevented everything. Months have been lost, and some of the uranium has gone to Iran!

3) Concerning the explosion of the train in Iran, there were *17 wagons of TNT, destined to Afghanistan!*

4) Concerning Tehran's atom bomb program, I can't hardly add anything. Everything is coming out as we discussed.

Best regards,
Ali
Paris, February 19, 2004

February 22, 2004

Dear Curt:

I send you below the real absolute reliable figures of the election in Iran:

Ghom:	4.8% (lowest participation)
Tehran:	9.3%
Kerman:	15%

Average all Iran 9%–11% total participation in elections.

The Minister of Interior, who is in charge of election, has refused to sign and proclaim the inflated figures as accurate.

On the order of Khameni, Hassan Rouhani, the General Secretary of the Security Council, proclaimed the results! It is as if

Madame Condoleeza Rice would proclaim the United States election results.

In Tehran, there were 12,000 mobile vans of the Mullah Mafia! This is using advanced technology by thugs to win the elections.

We have made detailed calculations to try to figure out the support of the regime.

Among those who have voted, if we take into account those who for any reason had to vote, like: military, Sepah–Basij, government employees, Education Ministry employees, participants to enter higher education, those receiving religious assistance, we arrive at the figure of 1.4 percent. This figure is the same as a poll taken by Mr. Abass months ago. He was arrested and put in jail.

Best regards,
Ali
February 22, 2004

12

ALI REPORTS

17–25 March 2004

"After the terrorist attack in Madrid, Khameni had a meeting with his inner circle. They had a party, everybody congratulating the leader for the success."

—Ali

THE MARCH REPORTS COVER A BROAD range of issues. Of particular
interest is the March 17 report, which describes in some detail
Tehran's plans for destabilizing Iraq and creating the conditions for
replacing democracy with an Islamic republic. Additional highlights:

- Iran's atomic bomb program, and plans to hide it from United
  Nations inspectors.

- Concerns in Tehran that the United States might discover that
  Osama bin Laden is hiding in Iran.

- A secret "Islamic Vatican" for promoting terrorism.

- German contributions to Iran's nuclear weapons program.

- Tehran's confidence in its ability to win the war in Iraq.

Dear Curt:

After the terrorist attack in Madrid, Khameni had a meeting with his inner circle. They had a party, everybody congratulating the leader for the success.

This is the comprehensive plan of the Islamic Republic of Iran for Iraq in the coming months:

3 Principal goals

a) Destabilization of Iraq

b) Create the conditions and structuring of an Islamic Republic

c) Contribute to the defeat of President Bush in the presidential elections.

In order to keep officially the regime out of the picture and deny any official responsibility the foundation of Imam Reza in Mashad *(Khoressur)* has been put in charge of the execution of the plan.

The Imam Reza Foundation is the most important foundation in Iran; relying on the religious center of Mashad. Unlimited ownership of land, agriculture, industries, real estate, trade, income from the religious establishment, most of the trade with former states of the Soviet Union and Asia, large interests and investments in Dubai. Net profits for the first six months amounted to the equivalent of $9 billion.

a) A first budget of $300 million has been allocated for the execution of the plan in Iraq.

b) 179 companies have been created for commercial–financial— investments in Iraq.

c) The areas targeted are: Karbela—Najaf—Kufe—Basra—South Iraq.

d) The activities of the companies are aimed at expanding Iran's presence—influence—structures in Iraq, the model being South Lebanon, Hezballah and all its political andsocial organizations and charities, social services and assistance, all controlled by Iran.

The comprehensive plan has 2 phases:

Phase I, until July 2004.

Phase II, after July 2004.

A) *Phase I.* Investments and trade are aimed at:

Agricultural land, purchases also of existing gardens and plantations, land for industrial zones, all land around shrines, real estate in any available form, (mainly around shrines), ships, hotels. Establishment of Charities for social services.

Investments in ports in South Iraq.

Supply of all kind of goods from Iran

This infrastructure should enable Iran to mobilize the people when it decides to start large scale protests and demonstrations, which is foreseen after July.

B) *Terrorist attack*

- No attack on Iraqi civilians (like Karbala)

- Attack on Iraqi security forces, police, etc.

- Attack on coalition forces

- Attack on foreigners involved in any activity

- Attack on foreign institutions

- Attack on bridges, water and electricity installations, and pipelines.

- Attack on coalition interests in *Iraq and abroad*, hoping that countries will withdraw their troops from Iraq and the United States will be isolated.

Phase II—After July.

- All the attacks mentioned in Phase I will be increased and intensified.

- Demonstrations, strikes at large scale are planned.

- Everything will be done to undermine the signed agreement and constitution.

- Everything will be orchestrated in such a way that the instability has the maximum impact on the presidential election, to defeat President Bush.

In this context may I mention that the decision to control the border with Iran is certainly a good decision, but we should not forget that the manpower and materials are already in Iraq.

Concerning Iran's atomic program, the game of buying time continues and Iran is going ahead with work. Hassan Rouhani's trip to Japan is a repetition of the game he played with Europe.

He is promising Japan economic benefits and asking Japan to intervene, so that more time is given Iran.

Tehran has made all the necessary arrangements to move its equipment, if necessary, when the experts of the UN atomic agency want to visit the sites.

Have no doubt whatsoever, Iran will be soon member of the atomic club!

Last week Khatami was asked by a journalist about Iran's atom program, his answer was: "There is a puzzle. I have to talk to President Putin." Our source tells us about the puzzle:

a) Iran has received a letter from Russia, stating that the atomic plant in Bushehr can't be finished on schedule.

b) A Russian company had sold Iran land–sea missiles; the first delivery has been done; but the missiles have no *chargeur*!

[PARAGRAPH DELETED]

[PARAGRAPH DELETED]

May I summarize for you the purpose of this call:

Analysis of the questions shows that two issues were on their minds and they wanted to know the extent of knowledge abroad about:

A) Iran's atomic bomb program

B) Al Qaeda—Bin Ladin.

a) *atom:* atom bomb program, concealment, especially warheads, US policy and reaction.

b) *Al Qaeda—Bin Laden:* About whereabouts, location if US hopes to arrest Bin Laden before the US election?

My feeling is definitely that they worry what does the United States know about the presence of Al Qaeda in Iran!

Best regards,
Ali
March 17, 2004

Dear Curt:

Please find below some information I received from my source, with the promise of more next week.

1) A new organization has been created. Its model is "the European [illegible]." Khameni has the leadership. It has a board of 5. The idea has come from Bin Ladin. He proposed two years ago to Khameni to create "an Islamic Vatican." Membership is determined on the lines of European [illegible]. The organization is secret and promotes Islamic discipline and martyrdom for Islam. Members are conservatives, young and old. Today there are around 400 members. There is a weekly meeting.

   Goals of the organization:

   a) Destruction of Israel.

   b) Attacks against American an Israeli interests.

   c) Promotion of Islam throughout the world, mainly in Europe.

2) Germany is one of the bases for Iran's atomic bomb program. They are making many trips to Germany. These two persons are key figures.

   a) Dr. Moussaviau head of organization for industrial research.

   b) [NAME DELETED].

Dr. Moussaviau has stated: "Concerning our requirements for enriched uranium, they are fully now covered."

Another important person for the atomic bomb program is D.R. Ismalizadeh. He is working at atomic facilities in North Tehran. He belongs to the group working for Mr. Aghazadeh, head of the atomic organization of Iran. Iran is working hard on its atomic weapons program.

Tehran—Al Qaeda has come to the conclusion that with regard to the measures taken against the United States, it is almost impossible to attack by planes targets in the United States. Detailed studies have been made about how and where to attack targets within the U.S. by sleeping units presently in the United States.

Speaking to Intelligence officials two days ago, Rafsanjani stated: "We have used only 5% of our power and possibilities in Iraq. We will do whatever is required to destabilize Iraq, and oblige the United States to leave Iraq!"

Rafsanjani has said after the attacks two days ago:

a) We have shown the United States it has no intelligence to stop us.

b) We have succeeded, because the United States and coalition forces are accused of being unable to protect Iraqi lives.

c) The killings will create pressure from the masses, so that Sistani cannot calm and control the situation.

I have detailed information on Iran's view that Israel is not going to put at risk its security and existence and will act with regard to Iran's atom bomb program. Iran's atomic warheads are almost ready.

The decision by P. Bremmer to better control the borders of Iraq is OK. Unfortunately, the Iranian terrorists are now within Iraq.

Best regards,
Ali
March 25, 2004

13

ALI REPORTS

5–28 April 2004

"In a meeting, Rafsandjani expressed his full satisfaction
   with the developments in Iraq, saying the United States
   would have to do the same thing they did in Somalia, and
   flee."

—Committee of Nine

IN HIS REPORT OF APRIL 5, 2004, Ali reminds us that he warned us about the threat posed by Ayatollah Muqtada al Sadr "a whole year ago! No one was paying attention to him then." His complaint is entirely accurate. His report of one year ago is not repeated here, as it appeared in an earlier chapter. Additional highlights:

- Al Qaeda continues planning for attacks on the United States.

- The 9/11 Commission report is viewed in Tehran as weakening President Bush, making him possibly politically vulnerable to another big terrorist attack on the United States. A "fatal strike" on the U.S. before the presidential election is back on the table.

- Tehran bribes al Jazeera television.

- The report of April 23 describes Tehran's plans to help al Sadr fight the United States in Iraq.

Dear Curt,

With regards to the events in Iraq concerning the role played by Moghtada Sadre. I send you enclosed a copy of my fax *last year*. I had information warning of the role Al-Sadre is playing now a whole year ago! No one was paying attention to him then.

At that time people were saying Iran has no military atomic program, Iran is a democracy, Iran is cooperating in Iraq and in Afghanistan!

Very important: Tehran—Al Qaeda are working on attacks within the United States. We should be able to obtain details of this program.

Best regards,
Ali
April 5, 2004

Dear Curt:

Please find below the latest information I got last night. I can only recommend to take seriously this information, so that loss of innocent lives are prevented.

1) In a meeting, Rafsanjani expressed his full satisfaction with the developments in Iraq, saying the United States would have to do the same thing they did in Somalia, and flee. Citing a report of Sepah, which had foreseen the U.S. forces would arrest anybody with arms in Baghdad, he ridiculed the Americans saying, "In their presence arms are sold in the streets of Baghdad!"

2) Khameni had a meeting with his foreign policy advisor, Dr. Abassi, from the Foreign Ministry having reviewed the latest developments:

   a) In Iraq, Iran's involvement being more and more exposed and mentioned.

   b) In USA, the recent 9/11 hearings and President Bush coming under attack and accused for failing to act, it was decided:

Dr. Abassi should review with his experts the decision taken not to attack within the USA, because people would be mobilized around the President. But now with the problems the President is facing, such an attack could be "the fatal strike," (the Iranian expression), "Tir Khalass" for the Bush administration. Dr. Abassi was requested to submit his conclusions as soon as possible.

In this context one terrorist project is ready and has been coordinated with Al-Qaeda. Execution needs only the political decision in Tehran.

As I told you, $70 million have been paid on the orders of Khameni for supporting anti-U.S. operations by Mogtader Sadre.

$12 million are being made available to "Iran's man" in the television Al-Jazeri. Al-Jazeri reporting is being coordinated with Tehran television.

(Information of tonight)

Background of terrorist actions and hostage taking: The comprehensive plan was formulated in May–June 2003. Details were given at that time to the Ministry of Defense.

a) On March 18, 2004, the establishment of 56 centers of intelligence and action in Iraq was finalized and declared ready for action.

b) On March 24, 2004, orders for hostage taking were issued.

c) 26, "experts" for hostage taking from Hezballah Lebanon are now in Iraq for hostage taking.

Rafsandjani in a speech to the charity organizations tonight and Safavi (Head of Guardian of Revolution) has declared to both that the United States will be defeated in Iraq.

Best regards,
Ali
April 12, 2004

Dear Curt:

On April 21, the representative of Moghtada Al Sadre was in Tehran asking for assistance.

In the meeting chaired by Khameni it was decided:

1) Any help needed should be made available to him

2) All the terrorist forces: Iranian—Al Qaeda—Islamic Jihad—Hezballah have been put on alert and mobilized.

3) Should there be any attack by the United States in *Najaf*—terrorist attacks will be carried out against American interests from *Turkey and throughout Europe.*

4) Special commandos from Iran are in place in South Iraq—Shiite areas to act in support of the terrorist actions.

5) "Any action required "will be taken against Sistani and Hakim, should they take a position against Moghtada Al Sadre.

6) Everything shall be done to prevent stability in Iraq.

It seems to me the coalition forces have to get rid of Moghtada Al Sadre. As long as he is in Najaf, he will create trouble and finally do what I mention above.

With my best regards,
Ali
April 23, 2004

Dear Curt:

1) In my fax of April 23, 2004, I mentioned the planning of terrorist attacks throughout Europe. Khameni has issued an order that the first attack should be on Germany. The planning and execution is being done in the joint committee of coordination Iran—Al-Qaeda.

2) It has been decided to explode an American commercial plane in the air. Most probably a plane taking off from Turkey.

3) I confirm again a terrorist attack within the United States is planned before the American elections.

4) I informed you that Tehran has made available $12 million to their spy in Al Jazeera; now a unit has been set up in Iran's television, which is coordinating around the clock their poisonous propaganda with Al-Jazeera.

5) Khameni has instructed Ayatollah close to him (Ayatollah Lam Karami) to issue a Fatwa, calling for worldwide Jihad against United States if Najaf is attacked. They hope the

choice of these Ayatollahs might, in an indirect way, conceal the official role of Tehran.

6) There is some unrest among members of Sepah, who have not the required Islamic credentials. Some of the highest level have been arrested and two of them have been executed.

Best regards,
Ali
April 28, 2004

14

ALI REPORTS

3–29 May 2004

"We have a bomb of 130–150 kilograms ready, a second
  one being prepared. The use of it in any town would kill
  more than 100,000 people."

—*Sepah Report to Ayatollah Khameni*

THE REPORT OF MAY 3, 2004, is of special interest, as it describes Iranian development of a missile warhead capable of mass destruction. Whether the warhead is nuclear or biological is unclear. Given the weight and alleged capabilities of the weapon, it is probably not a chemical or radiological weapon. Other matters:

- Bin Laden is last seen by Ali's agents "in a villa near Karadj."

- Iranian agents are crossing into Iraq from a base near Kermanshah.

- Al Zarqawi lunches with Sepah and al Qaeda after the beheading of an American contractor by agents of Iran's Revolutionary Guard.

- A plot to assassinate Ayatollah Sistani.

- In the May 20 report, the Committee of Nine is still divided on whether to attack the United States homeland.

- In the May 29 report, Ayatollah Khameni gives terrorists a "free hand" to proceed with attacks on America.

Dear Curt:

1) In my fax of March 17, after the terrorist attacks in Spain, I mentioned the triumphal reaction and congratulations at the meeting with Khameni. Khameni expressed the hope Tehran would have in the near future other more important success.

2) A few days later most of the engineers of the organization of the Army and Sepah were summoned and sent to a secret location. (We think close to Isphahan). They are denied all contact with their families. In addition there are also 80 foreign experts working with them. They are working on the Shahab missile and two warheads for this missile. The program is expected to be finalized within four months. The missiles are considered by Tehran more important than those of India and Pakistan.

   Tehran believes once exposed and shown, these missiles would send a "strong message to U.S.—Israel—Europe."

3) In a report submitted by Sepah to Khameni it is written: "We have a bomb of 130–150 Kilograms ready, a second one being prepared. The use of it in any town would kill more than 100,000 people."

4) Iran has helicopters with a missile having a range of 5–8 kilometers. Efforts are under way to increase the range.

5) There is a joint base of Sepah and the Army close to Kermanshah. From this base, commandos are sent into Iraq.

6) The last information we have about Bin Laden is that four months ago he was in a villa near Karadj. We don't know where he has been moved.

7) In report submitted to Khameni by his foreign military advisor, mentions a meeting last year in the United States at which

Iran's opposition, tribes, etc., were present. Financial assistance was promised, but only the Kurds have got financial aid

Best regards,
Ali
May 3, 2004

Dear Curt:

Abbu Massab Alzrghavi had lunch on Tuesday with heads of Sepah and other Al-Qaeda members.

The beheading of the American contractor was done by a special unit of Revolutionary Guards. Their training is,

a) Anti-riot.

b) To act in the war behind enemy lines.

Best regards,
Ali
May 13, 2004

PS: A large quantity of those arms used these days in Gaza against Israeli tanks has also been sent by Tehran into Iraq.

Attention: Congressman Curt Weldon—Confidential— Urgent—Only for your eyes.

Dear Curt,

Three days past was a very important meeting with Khameni. It was decided that with regard to the difficulties of the coalition in Iraq, everything shall be done to destabilize Iraq and throw the Americans out of Iraq.

Top priority: The killing of Ayatollah Sistani.

If I can give my opinion: the coalition should remove Ayatollah Sistani. His killing would create big problems. He should be kept at a safe place.

Confidential

As you have seen in the news, two trucks with chemicals have been arrested in Jordan by the security forces.

They had been sent through Syria to Jordan. According to the Jordanian authority, if exploded they would have killed more than 20,000 people.

Tehran has now *12* of these trucks with chemicals in Iraq. Arrangements have been made to bring further *13* to Iraq. A total of 25.

The planned attack with these chemicals will take place later, at a time when President Bush will not have the time to react, being left with a large number of deaths. Tehran believes this action will have the result that President Bush will lose the election.

1) Since the victory of the hardliners in the election and the decision of Khameni to impose a fully controlled and uniform political–religious system and all political–religious power centers submitted to him, a special advisory committee to Khameni has come up with a proposal to which Khameni has reacted favorably. To appease the population and give the impression of better governance, it is contemplated to have a no religious as the next president. For this post, Larijani, former Head of Television is envisaged.

Of course, Rouhani is reacting very negatively.

2) With regard to the events in religious places in Iraq. (Jajaf—Karbala—Kufe), Khameni has issued terrorist attack orders on American interests, in and outside Iraq.

3) Concerning terrorist attack within the United States, no final decision has yet been reached. Discussions are still taking place between those arguing an attack would mobilize the population around the president, and those believing President Bush has such difficulties that an attack would finish him. Decision expected to be taken next week. We shall inform you.

4) In a report submitted by the Air Force of Sepah to Khameni and the coordination committee with Al-Qaeda, confirming the possibility of a terrorist attack by a plane on the United States, it is said in the report that air control within the United States is such that it leaves 9–11 minutes for maneuvering before any plane is intercepted by the United States Air Force.

5) Khameni has again stated that, "There shouldn't be any negotiations with the United States. Such negotiations are useless and against our interests. We will take care that this boy [President Bush] is not re-elected."

Best regards,
Ali
May 20, 2004

Dear Curt,

Please find enclosed the latest information

1) Khameni has issued the following definitive order:

a) Iran's atom bomb program should be pushed ahead at full speed.

b) There is no need anymore to hide anything.

c) Experimental explosion should be done

d) Iran will not carry out its agreement and commitments with atomic agency in Vienna and will withdraw from the agency.

(The military and technical organizations working and mobilized on this project have asked for another month)

2) Khameni has issued the permission and given free hand to the coordination committee

Islamic Republic—Al Qaeda in Tehran for suicidal attacks on American targets in the United States and abroad.

3) Khameni has called a very important meeting on Tuesday with his close advisors and executives to review, finalize, and coordinate a comprehensive program against the United States.

4) A high level delegation headed by a general from North Korea was recently in Tehran. Both countries have signed an important military agreement.

Best regards,
Ali
May 29, 2004

15

ALI REPORTS

June–August 2004

"In a meeting, in the presence of Khameni...a possible attack of Israel against Iran's atomic installations was discussed."

—*Committee of Nine*

THE JUNE 2004 REPORTS DESCRIBE Iran making a crash effort to develop an atomic bomb. Isphahan is identified as the center of the A-bomb program, both in fact and by the slogan, "The first Iranian bomb is made in Isphahan!"

Fearing a preemptive strike by Israel to stop another "Islamic bomb," the Committee of Nine decides on a broadside of retaliatory options. These include launching sixty missiles armed with chemical warheads at Israel. Other highlights:

- Ali's warning of plans for a terrorist attack in Germany proves prescient.

- Ali pleads for CIA assistance, claiming he can get "exact locations and projected means" for planned terrorist attacks in Iraq.

Dear Curt:

We are witnessing in different areas the same policy, which is a clear indication that the policy maker is the same.

The goal is to destabilize by terrorism and sabotage the targeted country. This prevents reconstruction and creates conditions so that afraid foreigners leave the country.

This is what we are witnessing now in Afghanistan. The recent killing of a member of Doctors without Borders and members of charity organizations is the execution of this policy.

For this policy Khameni has made available $10 million in Afghanistan to the "Union of Islamic Leaders."

Following the payment of $10 million, The Union of Islamic Leaders issued an official statement that, "Kharzai is against God and should resign within 5 days!" In the framework of this policy, Hekmatyar is moving assets to the North–South–East, to destabilize the country for the elections.

Best regards,
Ali
June 6, 2004

Dear Curt:

It was in the news last night "Mail bomb hurts 17 in Cologne, Germany." Details aren't yet available. However for the record, find enclosed the fax I sent you April 28, 2004, that warned of this terrorist attack.

I confirm again everything I have written you about terrorist attacks against American interests abroad and within the

United States. If there was some "cooperation" from the CIA we could get the details.

Concerning Iraq, I repeat, attacks shall take place that it is even difficult to imagine. You have certainly seen in the news that two days ago, 40 Iranian terrorists with their weapons were arrested at the Iran–Iraq border.

Best regards,
Ali
June 10, 2004

June 17, 2004

Dear Curt:

Khameni has declared the defeat of President Bush top priority. He believes that an oil price above $50 dollars per barrel would contribute to such a defeat. For this purpose a comprehensive plan has been prepared to disrupt the flow of oil. In addition to Iraq, several oil centers, production and pipelines will be attacked.

There is no chance to protect by usual means the chosen targets. If we get financial assistance we would give exact *locations* and projected *means* for the attack.

I hope the opportunity will not be lost again, leaving afterwards everybody with regrets!

Atom Bomb. The enrichment process is going at full speed ahead. In our previous fax we mentioned that a large number of Iranian technical experts and foreign experts have been mobilized at a site, with no possibility of contact with their families.

The center is Isphahan. Seventeen enrichment units are at work. The program is to have a bomb within 6 months. The slogan is:

"The first Iranian bomb is made in Isphahan!"

In a meeting, in the presence of Khameni, with Intelligence, Security, Guardian of Revolution and Army, the rumors of a possible attack of Israel against Iran's atomic installations was discussed. It was decided in the case of such an attack:

a) 60 Scuds with chemicals would attack Israel.

b) Throughout Europe Israeli targets would be attacked.

c) Especially Synagogues.

d) Naval targets would be attacked.

The head of terrorist actions in Iraq has informed Khameni that during 10 days, 12 suicide attacks will have been carried out. He has been congratulated by Khameni.

Khameni has allocated $3 billion for a new project to control the population. In each part of the town, the mosque will play a role of intelligence—control—security and will have armed militia at its disposal, with power of arrest. This is in addition to Basif and Guardian of Revolution. The model of the Taliban in Afghanistan is being used for this setup. The regime hopes to crush any protest and opposition.

We had informed you that a United States desk has been created. Mr. Abasi, who is a close adviser to Khameni on issues related to United States, has been ordered to be involved closely with the desk.

My friend [NAME DELETED] sends you his best regards with the message: "If my proposals for Iraq had not been prevented by CIA, we would have saved the lives of a large number of patriotic and courageous American soldiers and innocent Iraqi people."

Concerning the situation in Iraq, I repeat, Iran shall do whatever it can to prevent any stabilization in Iraq.

Dear Curt, may I send you, for the record, the fax I sent you on Iraq months ago.

Best Regards,
Ali
June 17, 2004

Confidential—Only for your eyes

Dear Curt,

In a meeting with heads of Guardian of Revolution close to him, three days ago, Khameni stated: "I had a dream last night. Imam Mahdi (the 12th Imam) told me: "You should strike the USA within the United States!"

Khameni has issued the permission to act. With your cooperation and help, we can find out location and date.

Best regards,
Ali
June 30, 2004

Dear Curt,

Following our discussions last night:

1) Alzrghavi—the Jordanian terrorist—has been taken to Iran.

You can get all the details (date, whereabouts, etc.) from [NAME DELETED].

2) Khameni has gone with his close aides and the Mafia of terrorist acts to Mashad. They are trying by all means to interfere in Afghanistan. Even the General Prosecutor–killer Mortazavi is in Moshad..

3) As I mentioned to you before *"Mogheimie"* the biggest terrorists in Iraq, are executing the terrorist actions.

Best regards,
Ali
August 10, 2004

16

ALI REPORT

23 September 2004

"Khameni has congratulated the group working on the
atomic bomb, telling them two bombs should be made
ready the first of January of 2005, 'otherwise they
couldn't be considered as true Muslims.'"

—*Ali*

PLEASE NOTE, IN READING THIS BOOK, that there is a sharp drop in missives from Ali in the summer of 2004.

We talked in September and November 2004. Ali was deeply discouraged. His personal assets and credibility were nearly exhausted, spent bribing and begging information from his sources in Iran.

Ali reminded me—I did not really need to be reminded—that the information he is providing is merely a sample of much better, more significant, and detailed, intelligence that could be obtained. His sources expected him to use their secrets to buy a working relationship with the CIA, which has the resources to pay them "real money." Ali complained that, after eighteen months, no progress had been made with the CIA. The CIA was indifferent, and even hostile, to his offer.

After eighteen months of futility, Ali feared that his sources in Iran were beginning to doubt his promises that a working relationship with the CIA was "just around the corner."

Ali hoped that the new CIA director, my friend Porter Goss, might be willing to work with him. Would I talk to Mr. Goss? I did not need to be persuaded. I told Porter about Ali when he was chairman of the

House Permanent Select Committee on Intelligence. Now that Porter was director of the CIA, I planned all along, and as soon as possible, to remind him of the "Ali Affair."

My meeting with the new CIA director would more likely be successful if I could offer him some fresh intelligence. I asked Ali, "Can you get me some real dynamite?" A week later he was back, holding a stick of dynamite intelligence. I cannot disclose here what Ali told me, except to say that it was "actionable intelligence" on something at a specific location in Iran of such high priority that it was worthy of the attention of the president. Ali swore to me, "I stake my reputation that this is true."

That day, I arranged an emergency meeting with Porter Goss at CIA headquarters. Porter, upon getting Ali's "stick of dynamite," swung into action immediately. He would use every resource to "check it out." I reminded Porter of the "Ali Affair." He remembered. I described the gross incompetence and terrible missed opportunities I had experienced over the past eighteen months trying to get the CIA to do the right thing and work with Ali. And then Porter expressed his own deep frustration with the CIA and the intelligence community, saying, "Now you know what I have been up against."

There was a brief silence between us. And in that moment I understood instantly that not even the chairman of the House Permanent Select Committee on Intelligence, and not even the director of the Central Intelligence Agency, had the power to control the deeply entrenched and obdurate bureaucrats who really run the intelligence community.

The valiant Porter Goss, and his small band of champions from the House intelligence committee, are a tiny beachhead of reform landed on formidable shores, facing ominous odds. I fear they are fighting a losing battle. They need help. The president must help them. The Congress must help them.

And you must help them.

The CIA, DIA, NSA, FBI—the entire intelligence community—belongs to all of us. In the war on terrorism the intelligence community is our sword and shield.

We the people must fix it.

As I pen these words, it is December 4, 2004, a brilliant Saturday morning that seems to mock my dark despair. Ali has heard from the CIA—nothing but silence.

Dear Curt:

Following our discussion last night, please find below a summary of the latest information:

1) Khameni has congratulated the group working on the atomic bomb, telling them 2 bombs should be made the first of January of 2005, "otherwise they couldn't be considered as true Muslims."

2) The Shahab missiles shown yesterday in Tehran can fly more than 2000 kilometers.

3) Attacks on coalition forces in Iraq shall reach an unseen level in the coming days. Tehran is persuaded it can destabilize completely Iraq.

4) Khaled Marshal, the well known terrorist who was in Syria, has gone to Tehran.

5) Emad Mognie, the worst terrorist, well known to everybody, has gone to Iraq and is arranging the terrorist attacks.

6) The hardliners who control now also the parliament have changed Iran's economic policies. No liberalization and strong government involvement are being imposed by several laws approved by the Parliament.

Consequently, in a meeting with Khameni himself, the following decision was taken:

Whereas, before Tehran was thinking to follow the model of China, liberalization of economy and political controls, now with the change of economic policies, it was decided the best model for Iran is North Korea!

Best regards,
Ali
September 23, 2004

17

Conclusions and
Recommendations

WE LIVE IN AN AGE WHEN TECHNOLOGY has so empowered man that a
small group of terrorists—even an individual—could bring a nation to
its knees. For centuries only nation-states commanded such power.
Now nuclear, biological, and chemical weapons have made mass
destruction possible by merely pushing a button or breaking a vial.
The very technology that makes our civilization rich and complex also
makes us extremely vulnerable.

Civilization is at a disadvantage in the war on terrorism, as it is always
harder to build than to destroy. Sixteen centuries ago the Roman Empire
fell to barbarian invasions. Rome, with its cities, aqueducts, roads, and
far-flung commercial empire, became a victim of its greater economic
and social sophistication. The barbarians could sack cities and pull
down aqueducts more easily than the Romans could rebuild them.

Terrorists are the new barbarians. These new barbarians are far less
numerous than the barbarians of old, but hold the possibility of far
greater power in their hands because of the existence of WMD. America's highest priority must be to defeat the new barbarians. If we want
to avoid the fate of the Romans, we must stop the next, possibly catastrophic terrorist attack against the United States.

The penalty for losing to the new barbarians is obviously far worse than a sacked Roman city. Smallpox is a nightmarish plague right out of the Dark Ages, leaving its dead a mass of pustules. Nuclear radiation poisoning causes internal bleeding and every cancer imaginable. A high-tech electromagnetic pulse (EMP) attack, by paralyzing electronics, machinery, and basically shutting down everything, including the means for distributing, processing, and making food, could kill whole nations the old-fashioned way: by starvation.

Ali has offered to the intelligence community, on a golden platter, the means to stop the 12th Imam operation. The CIA, DIA, NSA, and FBI all refused Ali's offer. When, and by whom, will the 12th Imam operation be executed? What is this project? Will it be another attempt to destroy a nuclear reactor and kill hundreds of thousands of Americans with radiation poisoning? Will terrorists release smallpox or some other plague in American cities? Does al Qaeda have nuclear weapons? Does the recent *fatwa* by a fanatical Saudi cleric, giving Osama bin Laden permission to use nuclear weapons, signify the beginning of an operation to explode an atomic bomb in New York or some other large city? Worst of all, could the 12th Imam operation be an EMP attack against the entire United States, paralyzing the whole nation, and ending possibly with the death of two-thirds of our people by slow starvation?

Ali has intelligence not only on the 12th Imam operation, but also on other major threats to U.S. national security: Where is Osama bin Laden hiding? How are terrorists planning to attack U.S. forces in Iraq? What is the status of Iran's nuclear and missile programs? Who are terrorists targeting for assassination? Ali has proved that he has credible sources, which can help supply answers to these questions.

The intelligence community does not want Ali's help and is failing the American public. In an age when terrorists armed with WMD can threaten the very existence of Western civilization, we cannot afford to refuse help from any credible quarter. The intelligence community's stupidity in refusing to work with Ali threatens all of our lives.

However, the "Ali Affair" is not an isolated incident. Their failure to utilize Ali is just one more in a long string of major intelligence failures. The "Ali Affair" is a symptom of the fact that the intelligence community is profoundly dysfunctional.

The Clinton administration bears much of the responsibility for the incompetence of our intelligence community. The eight years of the Clinton administration coincided with the beginning of the post–Cold War era, when the intelligence community desperately needed resources and guidance to transform and reorient to face new threats, including the threat from terrorism. Instead, President Clinton slashed investment in intelligence, dropped the director of Central Intelligence from his Cabinet, refused for the first two years of his presidency to meet alone or even semi-privately more than once a year with his own CIA director, and ruthlessly pressured the intelligence community to support his political agenda, thereby corrupting the intelligence process.

There is also deep dysfunction in the culture and structure of the intelligence community that existed decades before the Clinton administration. The "Ali Affair" and the intelligence failures that led to the terrorist attacks of September 11 are rooted in the same causes. One cannot fully understand the intelligence failures leading to the September 11 attacks, and now to the "Ali Affair," without also understanding the general lack of vigilance toward U.S. national security that pervaded the Clinton administration and that made the tragic events of September 11 not only possible, but perhaps inevitable.

Clinton Administration Intelligence Failures

Outlined in this section are just some of the major cases, where there was an erosion of intelligence capability and abuse of the intelligence process by the Clinton administration.

WMD Terrorism. On Sunday, March 21, 2004, the press reported that a high-ranking member of al Qaeda claimed that the terrorist group had purchased a small "nuclear suitcase" bomb from Russia. These relics of the Cold War are small nuclear weapons, designed to look like a suitcase or briefcase. The Soviets planned to smuggle these sinister devices into the United States and detonate them near the White House, the Pentagon, and other strategic targets for the purpose of a surprise attack. One man armed with a "nuclear suitcase" could destroy a small city—a perfect weapon for a terrorist.

Ever since September 11, U.S. intelligence has taken seriously the possibility that terrorists might attack the United States with a man-carried "nuclear suitcase" bomb or other atomic demolition munitions. Indeed, according to the *New York Times* (see, "A Nation Challenged: Tip on Nuclear Attack Risk Was Kept from New Yorkers," March 4, 2002), one of the terrorist alerts was elevated by concerns that a "nuclear suitcase" might be *en route* to New York. We knew about the "nuclear suitcase" threat during the Clinton years, yet I could never persuade President Clinton or his Cabinet to take seriously the threat that a "nuclear suitcase" bomb might be in the hands of terrorists.

Seven years ago, I led a congressional delegation to meet with Russian general Aleksandr Lebed, then national security advisor to President Boris Yeltsin, who disclosed to us that Russia had developed "nuclear suitcase" bombs. Lebed said over 100 of these weapons were unaccounted for, apparently missing from the Russian nuclear stockpile. He warned these weapons might be in terrorist hands.

In August 1998 and May 1999, I chaired a series of congressional hearings featuring a prominent Russian scientist and former high-ranking Russian intelligence officers who confirmed the existence of Russian "nuclear suitcase" bombs. They all agreed with General Lebed that these weapons could have been stolen or purchased by terrorists. Yet the Clinton administration ignored these hearings and refused to participate. The administration resisted all my efforts, including an official letter to Secretary of State Madeleine Albright, to persuade it to query the Russians about the "nuclear suitcases."

Had the Clinton administration shown interest, I am certain General Lebed would have worked with us to get control of the "nuclear suitcase" threat, which now seems so imminent. Unfortunately, General Lebed is now dead. After surviving two assassination attempts, he was killed in a helicopter crash in Siberia in 2002.

With the death of General Aleksandr Lebed, a man who deserved our gratitude and respect, the United States lost perhaps our best opportunity to work with the Russians on eliminating the threat from "nuclear suitcase" bombs.

Ballistic Missile Proliferation. Based on false intelligence, the Clinton administration refused to deploy a national missile defense to protect the United States from rogue state or terrorist missile threats. Despite overwhelming evidence to the contrary, the Clinton administration insisted that, aside from Russia and China, no other actor could pose a missile threat to the continental United States for at least fifteen years.

The Clinton administration broke long-standing precedent by publishing an unclassified version of a new National Intelligence Estimate (NIE), the now notorious NIE 95-19. Normally, National Intelligence Estimates are not declassified for a decade or more. President Clinton's own former director of Central Intelligence, Ambassador James Woolsey, condemned NIE 95-19—written under his successor—as poor analysis, and has at least implied that it was the product of an intelligence process that was politicized to support the administration.

I commissioned the General Accounting Office to conduct a study of NIE 95-19, to assess the quality of its analysis, and to compare it to earlier NIEs on the same subject. The GAO report, *Foreign Missile Threats: Analytic Soundness of Certain National Intelligence Estimates,* found that the quality of analysis in NIE 95-19 was poor, and inferior to earlier NIEs on the same subject.

The GAO report provided the justification and the analytical basis for the establishment of a congressional commission, the "Commission to Assess the Ballistic Missile Threat to the United States." The so-called Rumsfeld Commission, named for commission chairman Donald Rumsfeld, concluded that NIE 95-19 had grossly understated the ballistic missile threat to the United States. The commission found that rogue states and possibly terrorists could pose a missile threat to the United States in as little as several years.

History proved the Rumsfeld Commission right, and the Clinton administration wrong. A few weeks after the publication of the Rumsfeld Commission's report, North Korea flight-tested in August 1998 a long-range missile with potentially some ICBM capability, thus making the long-range missile threat to the U.S. homeland a clear and present danger. Then in 1999, Pakistan and Iran both acquired medium-range ballistic missiles, ten years earlier than estimated by the Clinton administration's intelligence community. During these years, I chaired a series of congressional hearings trying to persuade the Clinton administration to change its policy on missile defense to match the reality of the emerging threat, to no avail.

The intelligence community had no alternative but to admit its error. Congressional Democrats joined Republicans in supporting my bill for a national missile defense, overturning, by a veto proof majority, the Clinton administration's policy against missile defense.

North Korean Nuclear Weapons Program. The Clinton administration falsely credited itself with halting North Korea's program to develop an atomic bomb by negotiating the 1994 Agreed Framework. Under the Agreed Framework, North Korea was to stop reprocessing plutonium from fuel rods at the Yongbyon nuclear reactor, in exchange for food, fuel oil, and the construction by the United States, South Korea, and Japan of two new, large (100 megawatt) nuclear reactors.

Yet the Clinton administration ignored open testimony before the Senate from its own director of Central Intelligence in 1995 that North Korea had already developed at least one atomic bomb.

Many of my congressional colleagues and I warned that the North Koreans were almost certainly cheating on the Agreed Framework and that North Korea was just buying time to develop a nuclear warhead that could arm the ICBM we suspected (correctly) was under development.

Moreover, the Clinton administration tried to mislead Congress and the American public into thinking that the big, new nuclear reactors, promised under the Agreed Framework, were designed so they could not be used to make atomic bombs. But testimony from leading U.S. scientists provided to Congress in March 1995 proved that these new reactors could potentially enable North Korea to develop 300 times the number of atomic bombs producible by the Yongbyon reactor.

In my capacity as a member of Congress's North Korea Advisory Group (NKAG), I contributed to a report delivered to the Speaker of the House of Representatives in November 1999. The NKAG report concluded that North Korea was cheating on the Agreed Framework, clandestinely pursuing an atomic bomb program, and probably was pursuing a uranium pathway to the bomb that did not require the Yongbyon reactor.

Three years later, in October 2002, North Korea admitted to the United States privately that it cheated on the Agreed Framework and was developing additional atomic bombs.

Russian Proliferation. The Clinton administration refused repeated calls by Congress to sanction Russia for missile and WMD technology proliferation. The administration claimed such sanctions would needlessly harm relations with Moscow, and were unnecessary because the Russian mafia, not responsible members of the Russian government, were involved in proliferation.

The Clinton administration even went so far as to suppress and cancel an intelligence program being conducted by the Department of

Energy—the "Russian Fission Program"—that did not support the Clinton administration's view of the Russian proliferation threat. In 1995–1996, I sponsored a congressional investigation of the cancellation of the Russian Fission Program. The investigation found that the Clinton administration had canceled the program—and had some of its best work destroyed—for political reasons.

In hearings, briefings, and numerous public appearances, I presented vast amounts of evidence challenging the Clinton administration's claim that Moscow was innocent of proliferating restricted technologies. Indeed, I publicly displayed actual missile gyroscopes and accelerometers from highly sophisticated Russian strategic missiles that had been supplied to Iraq and recovered by U.S. and international inspectors. These guidance systems, taken from Russia's most advanced and most carefully guarded missiles, could only have been supplied to Iraq with the connivance of Moscow. In March 1999, the National Intelligence Council—perhaps itself afraid to challenge the Clinton administration—invited me to speak on the threat of missile proliferation from Russia and China.

Now that the Clinton administration is gone, there appears to be a consensus that the Russian government, especially during the Yeltsin years, was deeply penetrated by the Russian mafia, and most major cases of proliferation had occurred with the knowledge and assent of Moscow.

Chinese Proliferation. The Clinton administration refused repeated calls by Congress to sanction China for proliferating missile and WMD technology, based on false intelligence. The Clinton administration claimed such sanctions would needlessly harm relations with China and were unnecessary because the alleged cases of proliferation had not occurred.

To protect its China-friendly policy, the Clinton State Department even went to such absurd lengths as denying the presence of Chinese M-11 missiles in Pakistan, despite clear evidence—including photographs—

the prohibited missiles were there. In ignoring the proliferation risk posed by China, the Clinton administration also loosened export controls, allowing China access to previously controlled technologies, including supercomputers that would greatly assist Beijing's nuclear weapons program.

As a consequence of the Clinton administration's reckless policy toward China, we now know that China did indeed export M-11 missiles to Pakistan, acquired U.S. supercomputers that could improve their nuclear weapon designs, acquired U.S. missile technology that could enable them to place multiple independently targetable warheads on their ICBMs, and stole advanced nuclear weapon designs from the United States. Some or all of these technologies could find their way to rogue states and terrorists.

India–Pakistan Atomic Bombs. The Clinton administration's general complacency about the proliferation of missile and WMD threats infected the intelligence community and led to one of the most colossal intelligence blunders in history: the failure to anticipate the nuclearization of India and Pakistan.

I was present at the intelligence community's open hearing on the global threat environment in February 1998, which was supposed to educate Congress on the issues of major national security concern expected to develop during the coming year. The briefing did not even mention the possibility of India or Pakistan conducting nuclear tests. Just three months later, however, India and Pakistan both tested A-bombs, surprising the intelligence community and the Clinton administration.

Subsequently, my congressional colleagues, including Floyd Spence, then chairman of the House Armed Services Committee, and I tried to convince the Clinton administration that their failure to anticipate the India–Pakistan A-bombs was symptomatic of their overall lack of vigilance toward the proliferation threat. The administration refused to listen to us, or to learn from experience.

Electromagnetic Pulse (EMP) Attack. The Clinton administration ignored the potential threat from EMP attack, based on a lack of, or false, intelligence. My congressional colleagues, Roscoe Bartlett in particular, and I were increasingly concerned that as missiles and nuclear weapons proliferated, rogue states and terrorists might use a nuclear missile to conduct an EMP attack. A single nuclear missile, detonated in outer space, could potentially destroy most electronic systems across the entire continental United States, paralyzing our civilian and military infrastructures. EMP could indirectly kill millions of Americans by causing the protracted failure of our infrastructures for supplying water and food.

Rogue states and terrorists might find EMP a way of getting the "biggest bang for the buck" since only a single nuclear missile, perhaps a primitive Scud launched off a freighter, would suffice to conduct an EMP attack that could devastate the United States. We were also concerned that evolving Russian and Chinese nuclear doctrines might be giving more emphasis to EMP attack.

Roscoe Bartlett and I conducted four years of hearings and briefings to gauge the Clinton administration's attention—and to try to provoke the administration to pay attention—to the threat from EMP attack. As a consequence of the hearings and briefings, we concluded that the Clinton administration was completely ignoring the EMP threat.

Indeed, during a congressional hearing that I chaired in July 1997, General Marsh, the chairman of President Clinton's "Commission on Critical Infrastructure Protection," while conceding that an "EMP attack could devastate the telecommunications and other critical infrastructures," nonetheless dismissed the threat as "so unlikely... that I do not believe it warrants serious concern."

Two years later, in May 1999, during NATO's bombing of Yugoslavia, I led a congressional delegation to Vienna (described in another context in the first chapter) to meet with our Russian counterparts from the Duma to see if Moscow could be persuaded to help resolve the Balkans crisis. During that meeting, the Russian delegation, angry at NATO's bombing operations, warned that Russia was not helpless, and raised the specter of a "hypothetical" escalation of the Balkans conflict into a Russian EMP attack that would paralyze the United States.

Subsequently, the House and Senate, by unanimous consent, established a "Commission to Assess the Threat to the United States from Electromagnetic Pulse (EMP) Attack." The EMP Commission delivered its report to Congress on July 22, 2004. The EMP Commission concluded that terrorists, rogue states, China, or Russia could make an EMP attack—and in some cases already had plans or were developing EMP capabilities—that would destroy the United States. In contrast to the Clinton administration, the commission found that the EMP threat deserved immediate and urgent attention, and offered a plan for protecting the United States.

Yamantau Mountain and Missile De-targeting. Although these issues are not related to proliferation or terrorism, they nonetheless deserve consideration as they highlight the Clinton administration's cavalier attitude toward national security, and toward truthfulness on intelligence matters.

It is a matter of public record that Moscow was, and still is, constructing a vast underground facility under Yamantau Mountain that appears to have no other purpose but to survive a nuclear war with the United States. This is not consistent with the new relations that the United States and Russia are supposed to enjoy in the aftermath of the Cold War. The Clinton administration refused to demarche the Russians on Yamantau Mountain. President Clinton even ignored the "Sense of the Congress on Yamantau Mountain" that I sponsored, and passed with bipartisan support, which urged the administration to seek an explanation for the Yamantau Mountain project from the Russians.

By pretending that the United States and Russia were already "strategic partners" and ignoring disturbing realities, the Clinton administration put at risk the development of future U.S.–Russian relations along a course of mutual honesty and trust.

As for the so-called "de-targeting agreement," the Moscow Declaration signed by President Clinton in 1994, it is no exaggeration to say that "de-targeting" was a fraud perpetrated by the Clinton administration on the American people.

Under the agreement, Russia and the United States were to "de-target" their missiles, so that the missiles were no longer aimed at either nation. Subsequently, President Clinton claimed over 100 times that the Moscow Declaration of 1994 had substantially reduced, or eliminated, the specter of a nuclear Armageddon that has haunted the American people since the beginning of the Cold War.

However, as a consequence of hearings and inquiries by Congress, President Clinton's own secretary of defense, William Perry, later admitted that missile de-targeting was unverifiable. Moreover, Perry acknowledged that missiles could quickly be re-targeted in a matter of seconds merely by pushing a button.

President Clinton was willing to lie to the American people, and perhaps to himself, that he had reduced or eliminated the single gravest threat facing the United States.

Purging the Best and Brightest. Many in the intelligence community heroically resisted the Clinton administration's political corruption of intelligence, and attempted to expose the lie that "all was well," when, in reality, the United States faced mortal threats. Many of these heroes paid by having their brilliant careers terminated by the Clinton administration, at great cost to our present national security. During the Clinton years, many intelligence officers, from all ranks, came to me, complaining about how they were being pressured to "cook the books." Many described the abuse of security investigations and psychological evaluations as a means of enforcing "politically correct" intelligence. I am certain that hundreds of our best intelligence officers resigned during the Clinton years in order to escape the noxious intellectual environment created by the administration.

For example, although he was not fired, Clinton's first CIA director, James Woolsey, resigned after two years because of his lack of access to the president. This was probably brought about in part by Woolsey's—and the CIA's—unpopular candor about the flaws of Jean-Bertrand Aristide of Haiti. In addition, Woolsey had refused to fire his capable general counsel—inherited from the first Bush administration—and to replace her with an unqualified Arkansas lawyer pushed by Clinton and his White House staff. Jim Woolsey was, in my opinion, and according to intelligence officers who served under him, the best leader and the most promising CIA director in twenty years.

There are other examples. Jay Stewart was former director of intelligence at the Department of Energy when he asked me to save a special intelligence program from being destroyed by the Clinton administration. Jay created the "Russian Fission Program," described earlier. It was one of the first intelligence projects to warn of a looming nuclear proliferation threat from Russia—a warning that proved prescient. Jay, a winner of the prestigious Bronze Intelligence Medal, was fired for defending the "Russian Fission Program," which was "politically incorrect" at a time when President Clinton was trying hard to portray his Russia policy as a big success.

Notra Trulock was director of intelligence at the Department of Energy when he came to me at the Cox Commission ("Select Committee on U.S. National Security and Military/Commercial Concerns with the People's Republic of China"). Notra discovered that a spy working for China had penetrated our national laboratories and stolen the designs for our nuclear weapons. But Notra found his investigation obstructed by the Clinton administration. The administration was trying to cover up China's nuclear espionage in order to preserve good relations with Beijing, and to avoid political embarrassment. Notra's brilliant career in the intelligence community came to an end when he did his job: he cooperated with the Cox Commission's investigation of atomic spying by China. Notra Trulock had been one of the most brilliant officers in the intelligence community when he was exiled by the Clinton administration, and unfairly pilloried by Clinton allies in the liberal press, for exposing China's spying and the Clinton administration's negligence.

Gordon Oehler was director of the Non-Proliferation Center at the CIA. He always told the truth to me and in his annual reports about the growing threat to the United States from ballistic missile and WMD proliferation. Gordon's reports were a constant irritant to the Clinton administration. His conscientious reporting of the facts about Chinese and Russian proliferation of nuclear, biological, chemical, and missile technology to rogue states tended to contradict the Clinton view that, because arms control supposedly works, a national missile defense is unnecessary. In addition to being a superb scientist, Gordon was a profound thinker on matters of arms control policy. When the Clinton administration finally drove Gordon out of the intelligence community, we lost one of our brightest stars.

John Deutch was universally respected as one of the brightest and most energetic members of the Clinton administration while serving as director of Central Intelligence. Deutch was on the short list of Clinton nominees to be secretary of defense. Then, Deutch made the mistake of honestly testifying to Congress that President Clinton's cruise missile strikes on Iraq had made matters worse in the Middle East. Shortly after Deutch's testimony, which angered President Clinton, the administration leaked embarrassing and confidential details of a secret investigation into security violations by Deutch. Deutch's careless handling of classified materials did warrant private disciplinary action, but should not have become a public media circus to assassinate the character and competence of a man who had served his country well. The leak forced Deutch to resign and ruined his career.

These are just a few stellar examples of how the Clinton administration purged many of the "best and brightest" from the ranks of the intelligence community.

All of this set the stage for the catastrophe of September 11. Given the intelligence community's poor track record, and the political corruption of the intelligence process during the Clinton administration, the intelligence community's failure to detect and stop the terrorist attacks on New York and Washington seems inevitable.

The 9/11 Commission and Congressional Intelligence Reform

President Bush and the Congress established the 9/11 Commission to find out: What led to the September 11 attacks? How could such a massive intelligence failure happen? What are the deep, systemic flaws within the intelligence community that need to be fixed?

The 9/11 Commission found three big problems in the intelligence community that contributed to the catastrophe of September 11 and that continue to imperil U.S. national security:

- "Stove piping"—The failure of intelligence agencies to share information with each other.

- "Group think"—A tendency in the intelligence community toward intellectual homogeneity, a lack of competitive analysis, a lack of diverse views and opinions.

- HUMINT—Weak human intelligence, too few spies, too much reliance on satellites, no sources penetrating al Qaeda or other terrorist cells.

The 9/11 Commission made recommendations to fix these deep-rooted problems in the intelligence community. The Commission's primary solution was to create an "intelligence czar" to be called the national intelligence director (NID). The NID has legal and budgetary authority to force the various intelligence agencies to cooperate and to share information.

But an intelligence czar cannot solve all of the problems in the intelligence community. Subordinating the agencies under a single director may well reinforce the dangerous proclivity toward "group think" by discouraging what little analytical diversity exists among the agencies. In the end, when the NID controls everyone's budget, all will want their intelligence to please the "czar." Predictably, controversial views that displease the "czar" will not long survive.

The president's Commission on the Intelligence Capabilities of the United States Regarding Weapons of Mass Destruction, which delivered its report on March 31, 2005, also had reservations regarding an NID. The bipartisan commission, which examined the intelligence community's erroneous reporting of WMD in Iraq and exonerated President Bush of charges that he had unduly influenced the intelligence community to lie about Iraq having WMD, called for deep and rapid reform of the intelligence community, but was not enthusiastic about the idea of an intelligence czar. The Commission pointedly noted that the NID was established "about halfway through our inquiry" and "became a sort of *deus ex machina* in our deliberations." "While we might have chosen a different solution," the Commission wrote of the NID, "we are not writing on a blank slate. So our focus has been on how to make the new intelligence structure work, and in particular on giving the [National Intelligence Director] tools...to match his large responsibilities."

The Commission also made many excellent recommendations for reforming intelligence collection and analysis, and for reforming the culture of intelligence, which are the root causes of intelligence failure.

Reorganizing the intelligence community around an NID is not the answer; there must be reform. The biggest problem with the intelligence community is not primarily its organization, but its culture and leadership. Does it make sense that, when an intelligence failure results in the deaths of 3,000 Americans, no one in the intelligence community is found responsible or fired? Furthermore, does it make any sense that, when "group think" contributes to the catastrophe of September 11, none of the congressional bills for intelligence reform make fixing the problem their highest priority?

"Group think" and the tendency toward intellectual homogeneity stem primarily from the way the intelligence community conducts analysis, not from its organization. These problems persist in the intelligence community because an "old guard" of managers and leaders continue to dominate the intelligence process. The "old guard" is adept at playing bureaucratic politics. They are good at firing "whistle blowers" and more competent intelligence officers, who might replace them. But members of the "old guard" rarely get fired. The bottom line is that if intelligence community managers remain the same, and if the culture of intelligence collection and analysis is not changed, the intelligence community will continue "business as usual." We will be as vulnerable as we were before September 11, 2001.

The following section describes what is really wrong with the intelligence community, and makes specific recommendations on how to fix it. The reader will find prescriptions for curing the deep dysfunction that infects the culture and structure of intelligence.

Our Intelligence Services Have Long Been Dysfunctional

During the Cold War, deep flaws in the culture and structure of the intelligence community often led to serious mistakes. For example, during the 1970s, the "B-Team," a group of independent scholars created by the U.S. government to double-check CIA analysis, found that the CIA fundamentally misunderstood Soviet military doctrine and was grossly underestimating the nuclear threat.

We now know that during the Cold War the intelligence community was wrong concerning the health and stability of the Russian economy and the longevity of the Soviet Union. Notwithstanding some claims by individual members of the intelligence community, the CIA and other intelligence agencies failed to foresee the collapse of the Soviet Union. This was a huge intelligence failure. Several problems are the source of our intelligence woes.

Group Think. Intelligence agencies and the intelligence community as a whole place a high premium on "speaking with one voice." The theory is that policymakers want "an answer" from individual intelligence agencies and from the intelligence community as a whole, and do not want to be "confused" with multiple, conflicting views. Advocates of "speaking with one voice" argue that the intelligence community is a practical arm of government, not an academic institution, and that offering a diversity of views would reduce the value of the intelligence community to policymakers. Intelligence managers fear that policymakers would not be pleased to hear a cacophony of voices from the intelligence community, but would prefer firm, solid, and single answers.

Consequently, intelligence agencies place a high premium on producing an "agency view" on major intelligence issues. Likewise, the intelligence community as a whole attempts to produce an intelligence community view—a single view that all intelligence agencies can support—in National Intelligence Estimates. Although National Intelligence Estimates and individual agency papers allow for dissenting views, these are discouraged and usually placed in footnotes. There is enormous pressure to keep dissent in intelligence products to a minimum.

Another motive for "speaking with one voice" is that intelligence agencies, like all bureaucracies, have vested interests. The outcome of particular intelligence issues often does have important implications for the size of intelligence budgets and for future opportunities for the various intelligence agencies.

What analytical and intellectual diversity exists within the intelligence community grows from rivalry between agencies defending their particular interpretations of intelligence that tend to support their own bureaucratic interests. There is tremendous pressure within intelligence agencies for analysts to conform to the corporate view. Indeed, analysts are already motivated to adhere to the corporate view, since their own careers depend on the success and importance of their particular agency.

The intelligence community and intelligence agencies impose "group think" on intelligence officers through a process called "coordination." Coordination attempts to build consensus within first an intelligence agency and then within the entire intelligence community.

At the agency level, intelligence reports must be coordinated; that is, submitted for peer review by all other analysts, who have an interest in the issue. However, the coordination process does not involve merely soliciting the opinions of others. Without corporate consent, the analyst cannot release, or publish, his paper as an agency product. Finally, once peer review is accomplished, the intelligence report then must be coordinated with managers in the branch, division, and office of the particular intelligence agency.

At the intelligence community level, in the National Intelligence Council where National Intelligence Estimates are produced, a similar process of coordination occurs. National Intelligence Estimates attempt to build consensus between agencies on intelligence issues. As noted earlier, dissenting footnotes are sometimes allowed, but strongly discouraged. The National Intelligence Council goes to great lengths to negotiate between the agencies so that differences can be blurred and a National Intelligence Estimate produced that speaks to the policymaker with "one voice."

The end result of "group think" and the coordination process is intelligence products that reflect the lowest common denominator of views within an agency and, at the intelligence community level, the lowest common denominator between agencies. In short, the result is mediocrity.

The coordination process explains why the intelligence community, though staffed with some of the most brilliant scholars and scientists in the nation, so often produces poor analysis, where sharp differences of opinion are softened or concealed, and the insights of genius watered down with the "common wisdom" of the average majority. The end product is usually bland, and often inferior to analysis produced by equally brilliant individuals working in academia.

"Group think" and the coordination process give rise to another evil, a sin associated with all forms of collectivism: no sense of ownership or sense of responsibility for the product. Collectivism does not breed even a sense of common responsibility for intelligence products. It breeds, instead, a sense of anonymity, and a sense of helplessness among individuals that they can have an impact on whether the product is ultimately good or bad.

How to Fix "Group Think." The destructive effect of "group think" is probably the single greatest weakness of the intelligence community. "Group think" can be countered by changing the analytical culture to give more emphasis to diverse and alternative views, and especially to encourage the replacement of "group think" with intellectual individualism.

We must restore excellence to intelligence analysis. The surest way of achieving excellence is by letting individual analysts have their say (with senior analysts signing their reports), and encouraging competing schools of thought.

In the late 1970s, the CIA, to its credit, recruited a team of outside experts to examine data on Soviet military and strategic nuclear doctrine, to see if a plausible or better interpretation of the data than that made by CIA could be produced. According to this "B-Team," the Soviets were more focused on war-winning strategies than on deterrence. In effect, the "B-Team" found that the CIA was "mirror imaging"—ascribing to the Soviet Union doctrines and strategies that closely resembled Western doctrines and strategies.

In the aftermath of the Cold War, we now know from examining Soviet and Warsaw Pact archives that the "B-Team" was right and the

CIA was wrong. Soviet plans for waging nuclear war were not just for deterrence, but also for achieving victory. Unfortunately, an embarrassed CIA never repeated the "B-Team" experiment, but we should make such "B-Teams" mandatory.

Pretended "Objectivity." Another serious problem in the analytical culture of the intelligence community is the pretense that intelligence community analysis and products are "objective" relative to policy. The intelligence community is supposedly providing "just the facts," pretending that it is merely supplying objective information to policymakers so that they can make wise decisions. The intelligence community holds that it is up to the policymaker to think through the implications of intelligence for policy, not its job to take sides or to bias the making of policy.

However, in practice, the intelligence community does have a point of view on policies. It is unrealistic to think that intelligence agencies and the intelligence community will not champion their bureaucratic interests through their intelligence products. They certainly report facts selectively, and "spin" facts, to support their point of view and to support their interests.

The intelligence community's pretense to "objectivity" would be less dangerous if they understood and acknowledged their own bias. But the fiction of "objectivity" is so ingrained in the intelligence community's view of itself that they are unaware of their very real prejudices.

Another problem with the intelligence community's pretense to "objectivity" is that it tends to harm the quality and usefulness of intelligence analysis. The intelligence agencies strictly forbid intelligence officers to take policy positions in their analysis. Intelligence community managers get nervous about reports that deal with issues directly discussing policy implications. Yet policy and its implications are the issues of greatest interest to the president and Congress.

Partially from fear of becoming involved in policy debates, the intelligence community prefers to deal with concrete material facts rather than abstract policy issues. So the vast majority of work in the intelligence community focuses on such "nuts and bolts" matters as, for example, the technical status of North Korea's nuclear and missile programs and "bean counting" the number of ships in the Chinese navy.

Usually, because intelligence community reports avoid policy and the "big picture," preferring instead "nuts and bolts," intelligence community products are far more useful to middle-level managers at the Pentagon and the State Department than to the President. The policy implications of the radio frequency of the Pechanga radar, for example, are not self-evident and unlikely to be understood by any president.

Thus, intelligence officers, sometimes the people in Washington best informed to offer policy advice, are prohibited from offering such advice. Moreover, because intelligence officers are discouraged from doing policy analysis, they are less capable of offering sound advice. Surely this situation does not contribute to our national security.

So fearful is the intelligence community of becoming entangled in debates over policy that direct contact between intelligence officers and members of Congress and their staffs is discouraged. intelligence community "rules of engagement" prohibits intelligence officers from taking direct phone calls from members of Congress or their staffs. So a member of Congress or other policymakers cannot simply telephone an intelligence community expert to ask a question. This situation defies common sense and the larger interests of national security.

Recommendations to Replace "Objectivity" with "Honesty." Policymakers would rather that the intelligence community be overt about political and policy views, rather than conceal these views behind a pretended "objectivity," and attempt covertly to influence policy through reporting facts selectively. If the intelligence community is overt about its policy preferences, it will make transparent any bias in the intelligence report, and help the policymaker weigh the credibility of the report.

Better still, intelligence reports should routinely present a spectrum of views and recommendations on policy matters. Intelligence reports could and should place intelligence in the context of its implications for policy, and make the best possible policy arguments for a spectrum of views—left, right, and center. The good policymaker will not blindly follow the recommendations of the intelligence community. Rather, this more thoughtful approach to intelligence, placing intelligence in the context of policy, will be enormously helpful to the policymaker in thinking through his or her own choices.

Finally, the intelligence community simply must take the initiative and provide strategic warning to policymakers, even if this means expressing an opinion on a matter of policy. The intelligence community claims it understood that international terrorism had declared war on the United States, and claims it did provide some warning in a single, short item that appeared in the president's National Intelligence Daily on August 6, 2001. But this is the equivalent of warning Franklin Roosevelt that the Japanese are about to bomb Pearl Harbor by burying a small news item deep in the Sunday supplement to the *New York Times*, after the sections on sports and entertainment.

Obsolete HUMINT Tradecraft. Intelligence community incompetence is especially marked in the area of human intelligence, or HUMINT. During the Cold War, defectors and intelligence sources from the Soviet Union tended to cooperate with the West for ideological reasons. The intelligence community in effect "owned" these idealists, and could call on them to do almost anything. The CIA could recruit HUMINT sources for often little or no reward, and even against their self-interests and at the risk of their lives.

The HUMINT situation has changed dramatically in the war on terrorism. Most potential intelligence sources will work only for pay, and do not see the West as the "good guy" in the struggle. Indeed, HUMINT sources tend to be Muslims, who are reluctant to aid the "Christian West" in what is thought of as a struggle with Islam on the so-called Arab street.

Yet the intelligence community continues to act as if the rules of the Cold War still apply during the war on terrorism. As in the case with Ali, they refuse to work with sources they cannot "own." They expect a degree of subservience and obedience that is unreasonable, such as demanding that the source trust the CIA completely and divulge the connections and contacts that are the only thing that make the source valuable. With these standards, it is not surprising that the intelligence community continues to be so unsuccessful in recruiting new HUMINT sources from the Muslim world for the war on terrorism.

Another serious problem with the present intelligence community leaders running HUMINT operations is they want to play it safe. Many of these people are near retirement and do not want to lose their jobs by getting fired or demoted for a politically embarrassing or controversial operation. These same intelligence community leaders have been affected by the long institutional memories of their agencies, reaching as far back as three decades to the Church Committee hearings in the Senate, which led to the first major gutting of our intelligence capabilities, or to the 1980s and the Iran–Contra Affair, and operations in Nicaragua against the Sandinistas.

The present intelligence community leadership has "learned" that being bold, daring, and taking chances in HUMINT operations can be dangerous to the reputation of the agency and dangerous to their own careers. To these intelligence community leaders, longevity in their jobs is more important than brilliant performance in the war on terrorism.

Recommendations to Renew HUMINT Tradecraft. "Aversion to operational risk" or "playing safe" is exactly the wrong attitude to take in the war on terrorism. HUMINT operations hold the key to victory or defeat in this war. We need new, bold leadership in the intelligence community willing to take the risks that are necessary to win.

We also need new intelligence community leaders who understand that HUMINT is now the most important weapon in our arsenal in the war on terrorism. Some of the problem with current intelligence community managers is, during the Cold War, HUMINT was not considered as important as technological means of collecting intelligence, like satellites and electronic eavesdropping technologies, termed SIGINT in the intelligence world. Indeed, judging from their behavior and budget requests, intelligence community leaders still have not learned, even in the midst of the war on terrorism, that satellites and SIGINT are less important than HUMINT in this new war. The key to renewing HUMINT tradecraft is new leadership.

Leadership. Far too many intelligence community leaders are incompetent, arrogant, and entrenched. This applies to leadership in virtually all areas: analysis, collection, and the development of new technology. Most leaders in the intelligence community and among the agencies rose to their position during the Cold War. They learned their craft during a different era and their ideas are now obsolete.

Perhaps more dangerous than the incompetence of intelligence community leaders is their arrogant and open hostility to President Bush, and to his effort to reform the intelligence community.

The arrogance of intelligence community leaders manifested itself during the presidential election when they virtually waged war against President Bush. The intelligence community produced intelligence just prior to the November 2004 election that they clearly hoped would help defeat the president. For example, the intelligence community issued an unclassified report—it is the usual practice for intelligence reports on a contemporary issue to be classified—proclaiming officially that there were no WMD in Iraq. It is hard to escape the conclusion that with this report, the intelligence community wanted to undermine President Bush's credibility for launching the Iraq War, and inflame antiwar sentiment just prior to the presidential elections.

Likewise, it is hard to see the book *Imperial Hubris*, by CIA intelligence officer Michael Schuer, as anything but a propaganda attack, or a disinformation campaign, aimed not against our real enemy, terrorism, but against a sitting U.S. president. *Imperial Hubris* argues that the Bush administration has committed a grave geo-strategic blunder by invading Iraq, and even in conducting the war on terrorism itself.

The fact that *Imperial Hubris* was published with the permission of CIA leaders is startling evidence of their hostility toward President Bush. CIA analysts are not allowed to publish books without first submitting their manuscripts for a pre-publication review, which can take months or even years. In fact, CIA analysts are actively discouraged from publishing books altogether and permission to publish is often not granted. Dr. Pry experienced a three-year delay before receiving permission from CIA to publish his book *War Scare: Russia and America on the Nuclear Brink*. In fact, he did not receive permission to publish his book until he resigned from the CIA and went to work for Congress. In contrast, *Imperial Hubris* rapidly passed through the pre-publication review process, and was enthusiastically endorsed for publication by CIA leaders. I believe this was because of its hostility to President Bush.

The arrogance and hostility of intelligence community leaders to the Bush administration manifests itself in their public defiance of administration attempts to reform the intelligence community. Intelligence community leaders are shamelessly leaking to the press, attempting to destroy the credibility of the new CIA director, Porter Goss, and his staff, who are President Bush's champions in the fight to reform the intelligence community.

The intelligence community is supposed to have a culture of secrecy. Yet the amount of public discussion about the internal affairs of the CIA is unprecedented, evidence that the old intelligence community elites have declared war on President Bush. The intelligence community, in its anger against President Bush and his reformers, led by Porter Goss and his staff, is resorting to character assassination, leaking damaging information from sensitive personnel files. For example, the intelligence community forced one of Goss's staff to resign by leaking that he had once been arrested for shoplifting a pound of bacon. Unflattering stories about Porter Goss himself, falsely linking him to assassination plots in Nicaragua when he worked for the CIA, have also been surfacing in the press, obviously leaked from intelligence community sources.

All of this is a ham-handed attempt by intelligence community elites to destroy Goss and resist Bush administration efforts at reform. If the Department of Defense engaged in such behavior to resist reform efforts by a Democratic president, the media would find such activities frightening and close to constituting an attempted coup d'etat.

Recommendations to Reform Leadership. The gross incompetence in the intelligence community over the last decade, combined with the current rebellion of intelligence community leaders, especially at the CIA, justifies a dismissal of present leaders in all agencies and across the entire intelligence community. The straightforward solution would be to fire everybody above the level of GS-15, which would eliminate virtually all the current senior managers. Firing everyone above the level of SES-1 would spare the most junior managers. Everyone remaining would move up, the lower ranks replacing the higher ranks, a new generation replacing the old generation.

A mass purge of the intelligence community could be quick and cause less pain than imagined. It would minimize the period of disruption— an important factor since we are now in the middle of a war on terrorism—and preserve a degree of continuity by promoting within the ranks, as opposed to imposing new leadership from outside. A selective purge would take longer, and could be more disruptive than the alternative just described, but it would preserve the best and brightest in the senior ranks, which have a track record of competence.

Contrary to the claims of intelligence community senior managers, who are openly complaining to the press, a purge of intelligence community management would not be a disaster. Naturally, the current crop of senior intelligence managers thinks that they are all indispensable. But I know from long experience working with the intelligence community, and from many close personal relationships with rank-and-file intelligence officers, that the vast majority of working intelligence officers would rejoice in the firing of managerial dead wood. "Regime change" in the intelligence community would benefit the rank-and-file intelligence officers who do most of the work, and who have spent their careers watching senior managers take all of the credit. Their views were well captured in this remark made by an intelligence officer to the *Washington Times* (November 19, 2004): "I can give them a whole list of people to fire."

Finally, when reforming the leadership of the intelligence community, we must not forget those among the best and brightest who have been exiled by the "old guard." They had the courage to stand up to the "old guard" and to warn policymakers about blunders and mistakes being made by the intelligence community. There are scores of former intelligence managers, who sacrificed brilliant careers to expose wrongdoing, who could give the agencies new leadership and have the qualities necessary to reform and renew the intelligence community.

Recruitment. An antiquated process for granting security clearances, necessary to hire intelligence personnel with skills vital to U.S. national security, can paralyze recruitment. Applicants for employment with the intelligence community must undergo extensive background investigations, and psychological and polygraph testing, before being granted the necessary security clearances. Typically, this process can take more than a year. Those Americans who have lived overseas for a protracted period of time have virtually no hope of ever being granted a security clearance.

The intent of the lengthy recruitment and security clearance review process is to ensure that only trustworthy individuals enter the ranks of the intelligence community. The security clearance process is intended to eliminate those who could be recruited by an enemy.

However, in practice, the long delays imposed by the recruitment and security review process is doing more harm than good. The process has the effect of excluding from recruitment Arab Americans and other ethnic groups who have language skills vital to winning the war on terrorism. One of the greatest weaknesses of the intelligence community is the dearth of skilled linguists in Middle Eastern languages; Pashtu, Farsi, and Arabic speakers are desperately needed. Nor are we able to train enough people to speak these languages fluently from among the ranks of current intelligence community employees.

The recruitment process, though well intentioned, is obsolete. Assumptions about what constitutes a "loyal American" are more appropriate to the Cold War and America of the 1950s, when the United States was more ethnically and religiously homogenous. Moreover, recruitment standards do not accommodate the reality that Americans travel more today or that many Americans are recent immigrants.

Recommendations for Reforming Recruitment. The security clearance process must be streamlined so that desperately needed talent can be recruited into the intelligence community to fill immediate needs in the war on terrorism. Top priority must be given to recruiting linguists.

The year, or more, currently required to grant security clearances to new intelligence officers should be halved to six months initially, and then further halved to three months. This can be accomplished by waiving that part of the background investigation that seeks interviews with acquaintances and neighbors from a decade or more in the past. Trying to trace a person's footsteps while that person lived or traveled overseas, especially when the foreign residency or traveling occurred years ago, also consumes vast amounts of time and resources. This too is part of the security clearance process that should be modified or discontinued.

The criteria for recruitment of intelligence officers must be broadened, made more inclusive, to reflect the ethnic and cultural realities of modern America. Recent immigrants constitute a growing portion of the national population, while Americans travel more, and many more have lived overseas. These Americans have the very skills in foreign languages and cultural knowledge most urgently needed by the intelligence community.

Admittedly, shortening the security clearance process and broadening the criteria for recruitment will increase the risk foreign agents may penetrate the intelligence community. But hostile foreign agents will penetrate the intelligence community no matter how stringent our recruitment process, a lesson we should have learned from the many successful Soviet spy operations against us during the Cold War.

Far more harm than good is being done to our national security by a recruitment process that prevents hundreds of loyal Americans with desperately needed talents from becoming intelligence officers while catching few spies. The recruitment process, as currently constituted, has the net effect of weakening our first line of defense in the war on terror.

Reforming the recruitment and security clearance process will take time, and probably not happen fast enough to meet our pressing wartime needs for intelligence professionals. In the interim, the intelligence community should rely more on contractors. For example, many jobs requiring foreign language translation could be outsourced as contract work. This would greatly lower the risk of penetration, as contractors would not be admitted directly into the ranks of the intelligence community. The intelligence agencies have vast experience working with contractors at arm's length. The pool of contractors would serve as a source of future recruits, and start hundreds of linguists and people with other needed talents on the road to becoming intelligence officers.

Inspector General Office. Within the intelligence community, every agency has an Office of the Inspector General or its functional equivalent. The inspector general is supposed to investigate allegations of wrongdoing, incompetence, or mismanagement within the intelligence community. The Office of Inspector General is supposed to be a safe haven for "whistle blowers," a place where intelligence officers can air grievances or give warning about managerial incompetence, without fear of harming their careers.

Unfortunately, the Office of Inspector General in most intelligence agencies has become the opposite of what was intended. Instead of being a safe haven for "whistle blowers," the Inspector General Office typically acts as "fly paper"—a means of luring, capturing, and suppressing "whistle blowers." Instead of being a fair arbiter between intelligence officers and managers, the Office of Inspector General has become an oppressive arm of intelligence managers, an undercover police force within the intelligence community intended to stamp out "dissidents" who might embarrass the intelligence community by exposing the truth about mistakes and mismanagement.

I am personally aware of cases where intelligence community "whistle blowers" have been wrongly subjected to psychological testing and counseling as punishment for speaking to the Inspector General Office. The Inspector General Office has even been complicit in the betrayal and persecution of "dissident" analysts. If the Office of Inspector General were working the way it should, the Congress would not hear so much about mistakes and mismanagement within the intelligence community from so many of the best and brightest intelligence officers.

The straightforward step of making the Office of Inspector General directly answerable to the House and Senate intelligence committees, not to intelligence community managers, can reform the Inspector General Office and make it what it should be.

Office of Congressional Affairs. Within the intelligence community, every intelligence agency has an Office of Congressional Affairs. It is supposed to serve as a liaison between Congress and the intelligence community, advertising itself as a means of making the intelligence agencies more responsive.

In practice, the Office of Congressional Affairs serves the intelligence community, and tends to view Congress as an adversary. It can treat congressional requests for information like foreign intelligence: requests are scrutinized for their political significance, possible implications and impact on agency interests, and their possible implications and impact on the Executive Branch. Nor are requests kept confidential. Indeed, on particularly important matters, or on matters involving great political sensitivity, congressional requests for information from the intelligence community are shared by the Office of Congressional Affairs with the Executive Branch, so that the report or briefing ultimately delivered to Congress can be "spun" in the proper direction and made "politically correct."

Another purpose of the Office of Congressional Affairs is to serve as a firewall between intelligence officers and members of Congress. Under the rules of engagement invented by the intelligence community, members of Congress cannot call or speak directly to intelligence officers without going through the Office of Congressional Affairs. The intelligence community justifies this rule by claiming that it wants to protect its analysts from "political contamination" by members of Congress. This is consistent with the intelligence community's avowed goal of "objectivity" on policy matters, a fallacy already discussed.

Here, too, there is a straightforward solution: abolish the Office of Congressional Affairs. Replace it with an intelligence community phone book so that members of Congress and staff holding appropriate security clearances will have direct access to all intelligence managers and analysts. This will make the intelligence community more useful and responsive to Congress, and increase the flow and timeliness of information to the House and Senate.

Congressional Oversight. Congress bears much of the responsibility for the dysfunction in the culture and structure of the intelligence community. Within Congress, the bodies responsible for oversight on intelligence matters are the House Permanent Select Committee on

Intelligence and the Senate Select Committee on Intelligence. Both congressional intelligence committees are stacked with former intelligence community staffers. These staffers remain loyal to their agencies. They tend to over-identify with the intelligence community, accept intelligence community explanations for problems, and are quick to defend the intelligence community against outside critics. Moreover, some members of the intelligence committee's staff hope to return to the intelligence community, and get new jobs as managers and analysts within the community. They hope to work with and for the very people they are supposed to regulate.

And it works the other way too. The intelligence community exerts virtual veto power on the selection of members and staff for the congressional intelligence committees. I have personal knowledge that the intelligence committees are very reluctant to take on members or staff who are not approved by the intelligence community. The bottom line is that oversight on intelligence by the congressional intelligence committees has been corrupted by this cozy relationship with the intelligence community. In fact, prior to the intelligence disaster of September 11, the most significant critiques of intelligence community performance came from the House Armed Services Committee, not the congressional intelligence committees. The House Armed Services Committee:

- Established the Rumsfeld Commission. The Rumsfeld Commission proved that the notorious National Intelligence Estimate 95-19 was analytically flawed and wrong about future missile threats.

- Investigated why the Directorate of Intelligence at the Department of Energy suppressed the "Russian Fission Program." The committee found that the Clinton administration had terminated the "Russian Fission Program" to suppress evidence of Moscow's complicity in the proliferation of missiles and WMD technology.

- Initiated and took the lead in investigating the intelligence failures that led to the terrorist bombings of the Khobar Towers in Saudi Arabia in 1996, and the terrorist bombing of the USS *Cole* in 2000, which killed dozens of American soldiers and sailors. As a member of the House Armed Services Committee intimately familiar with the Khobar Towers and the USS *Cole* investigations, I know that the primary goal of the House and Senate intelligence committees was to protect the reputation of the intelligence community. In the House intelligence committee's view, the single biggest issue in the Khobar Towers and USS *Cole* investigations was to resist having the final reports describe these tragedies as "intelligence failures."

- Established the EMP Commission. The EMP Commission found that the intelligence community wrongly ignored the threat of EMP attack to the United States from rogue states and terrorists and had grossly underestimated the threat from China and Russia.

Frankly, I am surprised that the press never took any notice of this historical record, which strongly suggests that the congressional intelligence committees are not doing their jobs, and that the House Armed Services Committee is providing the only real intelligence oversight. Unfortunately, the House Armed Services Committee can only report wrongdoing by the intelligence community. It does not have authority over the CIA or the power to reform the whole intelligence community.

Recommendations for Reforming Congressional Oversight. The House and Senate intelligence committees can become true oversight committees, if more staff came from the military and academia; if the chairman of the National Intelligence Council and all the national intelligence officers were chosen with the "advice and consent" of the House and Senate intelligence committees; and if intelligence community managers were responsible to Congress for competent management.

Grand Strategy for Winning the War on Terrorism

Intelligence is more important today than ever before because the enemy is decentralized, nearly invisible, and potentially armed with WMD. To stop a decentralized enemy, with a dispersed leadership and many autonomous cells, we must intercept and disrupt terrorist operations before they happen. That means preemptive operations to kill terrorist leaders and destroy autonomous cells, and intelligence that we can use to apply pressure on their rogue-state supporters. All this requires superior intelligence from our intelligence services.

The 9/11 Commission found that the failure of the intelligence community to work together was the primary cause of the security failure that resulted in the successful terrorist attack on September 11. As I described in the first chapter, I foresaw the need to make the various agencies within the intelligence community work together in 1999. This was two years before the terrorist attacks of September 11, 2001, and five years before the 9/11 Commission arrived at a similar conclusion.

On July 30, 1999, in a letter to then Deputy Secretary of Defense John Hamre, I proposed establishing a National Operations Analysis Hub, or "NOAH," to serve as a means of fusing intelligence from all agencies (also discussed in the first chapter). NOAH would achieve the kind of cooperation that the 9/11 Commission and Congress have advocated. I believe NOAH is still the best way of achieving joint collection analysis in our intelligence community to support preemptive operations and win the war on terrorism. (To read my 1999 letter to Hamre, I refer the reader to the appendix.)

The 9/11 Commission, and the congressional legislation that followed, believed an intelligence czar would force the intelligence agencies to work together. This is the wrong approach. NOAH would achieve collaboration within the intelligence community without the kind of disruption a "czar" will cause. NOAH, and intelligence fusion centers like it, can be added to the existing intelligence community, without massive reorganization. A Presidential Executive Order would suffice to establish NOAH and to compel the various intelligence agencies to share information and analytical capabilities. In addition to NOAH, the changes in intelligence culture and structure described earlier are all that are necessary to reform and achieve optimum effectiveness of our intelligence community.

We cannot afford, in the middle of the war on terrorism, to enact reforms that will do more harm than good, by disrupting our intelligence community and worsening its most dangerous proclivity, the tendency toward "group think." The 9/11 Commission and the Congress have butchered the intelligence community, when what is really needed is brain surgery.

Alliance with Russia: "New Times, New Beginning." President Bush, speaking in Halifax on December 1, 2004, in his first major foreign policy speech after re-election, called for global cooperation in the war on terrorism. According to the *Washington Times* (December 2, 2004), "President Bush...challenged international leaders to create a new world order, declaring pre-September 11 multilateralism outmoded and asserting that freedom from terrorism will come only through pre-emptive action against enemies of democracy." The president declared, "The success of multilateralism is measured not merely by following a process, but by achieving a result."

To achieve the results envisioned by President Bush in the war on terrorism, the United States should forge a grand alliance with Russia. A formal treaty between Washington and Moscow, resurrecting something like the anti-Hitler alliance of World War II, would be enormously useful to both nations.

Politically, a U.S.–Russia anti-terror alliance would greatly boost the morale of both sides and create a kind of coalition, which other states would be more willing to follow. Practically, it would achieve real military and intelligence cooperation of the sort necessary to win the war on terrorism, instead of the present lukewarm cooperation on intelligence that currently characterizes the U.S.–Russian relationship.

Russia would bring much to the table as an ally of the United States. An alliance established by treaty would provide a golden opportunity for both sides to achieve a real meeting of minds on containing Russian WMD technology and keeping it out of terrorist hands.

Russian national pride, wounded by the defeat in the Cold War, could scarcely resist a bilateral treaty with Washington, which would effectively recognize Russia as an equal of the United States, and restore at least some of Russia's lost superpower status and uniqueness in the world. Moscow would be willing to concede much to Washington to achieve such a treaty. Washington and Moscow both have a strongly shared interest in keeping Russian WMD secure. Nunn-Lugar and other non-proliferation programs have tended to treat Russia as a subordinate to the United States. A Washington–Moscow anti-terror treaty would afford an opportunity to redefine the non-proliferation programs of both sides in a healthier way that enlists Russian enthusiasm for the cause.

Beyond contributing to non-proliferation, Russia would bring many other important assets to an anti-terror alliance. Russia has the longest border in the world with the states of Central Asia, the breeding ground and homeland of international terrorism. Russia has hundreds of years of experience in conducting clandestine operations in Central Asia. Russia has an extensive intelligence network in Central Asia and the Middle East, probably more extensive than that of the United States. In the area where the United States is weakest—in HUMINT sources—Russian intelligence services are much stronger and have much to offer our intelligence community.

Last but not least, the Russian army, though poor in material resources, is battle-hardened and experienced in fighting terrorists in Chechnya. The Russian army could greatly ease the burden on U.S. soldiers in helping fight future wars against terrorists and for peace-keeping in places like Iraq. Moscow and Washington are natural allies in the war on terrorism.

Russia has been at war with international terrorism longer than the United States and has suffered numerous bombings and hostage takings on its home territory. Russia was right that the Chechens have more in common with international terrorists than "freedom fighters," and the United States was wrong to believe otherwise. It is now known that the Chechen terrorists worked closely with al Qaeda and supported terrorist activities in the Balkans.

The brutal terrorist attacks on Beslan in 2004 killed hundreds of Russian children. This was not an accident; the terrorists deliberately targeted Russian children. The Beslan massacre enraged the Russian people more than any other attack on their territory, raising emotions similar to those experienced in the United States after the September 11 attacks on New York and Washington.

I went to Beslan after the attacks to express my personal sympathy and to extend the hand of friendship to the Russian people. I was appalled that no one from the State Department was there before me and that the United States seemed slow in expressing sympathy and seeking common cause with Russia to avenge the terrorist attack. In the aftermath of the September 11 attack, Moscow quickly expressed its condolences to the United States. But in the aftermath of Beslan, there was no comparable official gesture of sympathy from the United States

There are indicators that Russia is seeking an alliance with the United States against terrorism. However, because of wounded national pride and a desire not to appear weak, Russia appears to want the United States to take the initiative. In the aftermath of the Beslan attack, the chief of the Russian General Staff, Colonel General Baluyevski, declared that Russia would preemptively strike terrorists anywhere in the world, using all military means at its command, "except nuclear weapons." Disavowing the use of nuclear weapons in the war on terrorism was clearly a big concession by Moscow to Washington. The United States has often and openly criticized Russian military doctrine for placing no limit on nuclear use.

Baluyevski's declaration of a world war on terrorism and endorsing preemptive operations against terrorists was a formula identical to the anti-terror doctrine used by the United States. Moreover, in the aftermath of the U.S. presidential election, Russian president Vladmir Putin applauded the American people for re-electing President Bush. Putin praised Bush, saying that the president "will not yield in the war against terrorists." It is hard to escape the conclusion that Russia is sending a signal to the United States that it is ready to join forces with America in the war on terrorism.

I have proposed a plan to the State Department for establishing a Washington–Moscow anti-terror alliance. Over the past several years, I have also been implementing a program, called "New Times, New Beginning," that would facilitate the establishment of a true friendship and strategic partnership between the United States and Russia. "New Times, New Beginning" has been reviewed and approved by the Russian Academy of Sciences and received the endorsement of President Putin.

"New Times, New Beginning" calls for cooperation between the United States and Russia on a broad range of scientific, cultural, economic, and military issues. The theory behind the program is that it will be easier to build trust between the United States and Russia by cooperating in areas less controversial, so that confidence can be increased and we can come to rely on each other for more important matters, such as joint military and intelligence operations.

The war on terrorism has created an opportunity for the United States and Russia to move swiftly toward friendship and cooperation on all fronts, making national security the centerpiece of the relationship with an alliance against terrorism. "New Times, New Beginning" will make it more likely that a U.S.–Russian alliance today will last beyond the war on terrorism, becoming real friendship and not just an alliance of expediency.

Our goal should be to draw Moscow further in the direction of democracy, and eventually make Russia a part of the West. This would be just as important an achievement as victory in the war on terrorism. If Russia joins the Western democracies, there would be no going back to the Cold War, and the future shape of world order will be so transformed in a direction favorable to democracy—leaving China as the world's only remaining major totalitarian state—that the ultimate global triumph of freedom would seem assured.

Liberation: Iran and the Ronald Wilson Reagan Institute for Freedom.
President Bush, in his second inaugural address on January 20, 2005, demonstrated boldness and vision when he proclaimed, "The best hope for peace in our world is the expansion of freedom."

Predictably, the usual media suspects denounced President Bush's speech as laying the ground for a reckless crusade. Ironically, President Bush's critics, who often posture as the champions of freedom and human rights, seem most vexed when the president agrees with them and wants to act. President Bush is absolutely right: Central to the U.S. grand strategy in the war against terrorism must be the promotion of freedom globally.

The promotion of freedom would be advanced greatly if we turn our attention soon to the liberation of Iran. Iran is the world's leading sponsor of international terrorism. We cannot win the war on terror as long as terrorists have a safe haven and sponsor in Iran. The United States will always be on the defensive as long as Iran is free to plot new terrorist offensives against the West. Iran is known to have played some role in most major terrorist operations against the United States over the last two decades.

The United States would be justified in launching a preemptive war against Iran. As we know from Ali, Iran sponsored the terrorist plot in August 2003 that was probably aimed against the Seabrook Nuclear Reactor. Iran presently is sponsoring terrorism in Iraq, killing U.S. troops and allies. Iran has made a strategic decision to destabilize Iraq, to turn the country into an Islamic republic or a haven for terrorists. In its undeclared war on the United States and on the Iraqi people, Iran is the enemy of freedom. All of this certainly constitutes a *casus belli*.

Yet, as we now know, there is more. Iran is on the verge of developing, or may already possess, the atomic bomb. We know from Ali that Iran violated the nuclear Non-Proliferation Treaty, and plans to violate any future agreement that might prevent it from becoming a nuclear weapons state. Intelligence provided by Ali, and Iran's past behavior, proves that Tehran will cheat on its recent agreements with Britain, France, and Germany, and will never give up its atomic bomb program. Iranian pledges to Europe and the United Nations that it will not develop the atomic bomb are unverifiable in any event. History suggests, as in the case of North Korea, that unverifiable nuclear agreements constitute a virtual guarantee that the suspected state will eventually get the bomb.

An Iran armed with the atomic bomb is an unacceptable threat to U.S. and global security. Iran already has missiles that can strike U.S. forces in Iraq and Saudi Arabia, as well as the state of Israel. Iran could give its atomic bomb to terrorists, who could then use it on the United States, perhaps detonating it in New York harbor.

Just a single nuclear missile launched off a freighter near the shores of the United States, detonating the warhead at high altitude, could achieve an EMP attack against the entire continental United States. The congressionally established EMP Commission last year warned that terrorists could perform such an attack. The Commission also warned that an EMP attack is one of the few means available to terrorists or rogue states for destroying the United States as a society. An EMP could paralyze all electronic systems across the entire United States, shutting down the infrastructures for power, transportation, communications, food, and water. A paralyzed United States would cease to be an industrial and military power, and millions of Americans could die of starvation. Through an EMP attack, terrorists could win their war.

Significantly, Iran has test-launched a Scud missile off a ship in the Caspian Sea. This launch mode is so inaccurate that virtually its only useful purpose is for EMP attack. Iran has also detonated missiles at high altitudes, in a manner consistent with testing the fusing of a warhead for EMP attack. Western analysts have described these missile tests as failures because the missiles did not complete their ballistic trajectories. However, Tehran declared these strange missile tests to be successful. If Iran were practicing for an EMP attack, the missile flights were successful.

The United States cannot risk the emergence of a nuclear-armed Iran. However, neither can the United States support another war right now. U.S. military forces are stretched thin in Iraq and Afghanistan. The United States is also on the cusp of another nuclear crisis with North Korea, and must be prepared for that eventuality. Consequently, war against Iran is not the answer. Regime change in Tehran will come from the Iranian people themselves, and might well be achieved peacefully.

Indeed, the Iranian people may be our best hope for freedom in Iran, and for the future security of the West. Ali's intelligence indicates that the Iranian people do not support the revolutionary government. Ali himself is part of a counter-revolutionary movement that is confident that it can overthrow the mullahs in Iran. Ali and his associates have shared with me a credible plan for achieving that end without war. They do not ask for, or want, U.S. military intervention or military aid. Iran's liberators would require only a modest amount of financial support from the United States.

A free Iran, Iraq, and Afghanistan would break this crescent of crisis in the Middle East. Freedom would convert these terrorist hotbeds into forces for progress, and examples of democratization for other states of the Islamic world. Americans should continue to support the spread of freedom to other nations and peoples as a means of making our own liberty more secure, as President Bush is doing in Afghanistan and Iraq, and as we as a nation have done since the end of World War II.

The expansion of freedom to Russia is drawing Moscow westward and makes U.S. liberty more secure. Democracy is still young in Russia. The democratic experiment in Russia could still fail. America needs to make a major effort to ensure that democracy succeeds in Russia, so that Russia can take its place alongside the Western democracies as a friend, and not lapse into authoritarianism. If freedom fails in Russia, Moscow could become an ally of totalitarian China, and the source of a new Cold War.

The liberation and democratization of Afghanistan and Iraq, if we succeed, promises to create a more stable world order, and to make our nation and liberties more secure against the threat of terrorism. Whatever our party affiliations, all Americans should support President Bush in this effort to bring freedom to Afghanistan and Iraq and to establish democracies in those societies.

Despite our long experience that bringing freedom to others also significantly increases our national security, the United States still does not seem to appreciate that the best preemptive strategy is the active liberation of other nations. If the bomb or missile existed that could provide to the United States the same level of security, as did the transformation into democracies of Germany, Japan, and the Soviet Union, would it not be wise to invest billions into that weapons system? Yet our investment in promoting political and economic freedom as a "weapons system" to defend our liberty is modest, especially considering its proven success. The National Endowment for Democracy, the Agency for International Development, and other small programs scattered in various federal agencies are an inadequate commitment to promoting freedom in the world.

Most of these programs are not integrated into a national security strategy. President Bush has done a heroic job in Iraq and Afghanistan, liberating those countries and attempting to reconstruct them as democratic nations. But reconstructing these nations as democracies is being done on an *ad hoc* basis. This is not the fault of the Bush administration. It is our collective fault as a nation for our failure to take more seriously the use of liberty as the most effective weapon in our arsenal to protect our own national security. We would be having a much easier time in Iraq and Afghanistan now if there were contingency plans on the shelf, planned out well in advance, for helping these countries become democracies.

Just as the United States has contingency plans for winning all manner of wars against all conceivable adversaries, we need contingency plans for winning the peace against possible adversaries, by transforming them into democracies. Right now, we usually find ourselves with no exit strategy after achieving military victory. There should be a standard exit strategy when we are compelled to defeat an authoritarian or totalitarian power completely, as we did in Iraq. Indeed, our national security policy should invest more resources in trying to transform our political adversaries into democracies before war becomes necessary.

Accordingly, I plan to introduce legislation to establish a new institute dedicated to the cause of advancing freedom in the world, and so making our own nation and liberty more secure. The Ronald Wilson Reagan Institute for Freedom would have area specialists dedicated to analyzing the prospects for creating programs and strategies to move authoritarian and totalitarian states toward freedom. The Institute would have on-the-shelf contingency plans for democratizing those countries as part of a larger national security policy in peacetime, and as part of an exit strategy in case the United States is compelled to defeat those nations in war. It would keep track of the activities of all agencies dedicated to advancing freedom. The Institute would propose ways to use the resources we spend promoting freedom more efficiently and effectively, and as part of a broader national security policy.

A new world order based on freedom is the ultimate weapon against terrorism.

Appendix One

Recent Letter from Ali

— 1 —

(6 Pages, this included)

Top Secret — Only for your eyes

Attention Dr. Peter Vincent Prey

Dear Peter,

Please find enclosed some very important informations.
As I mentioned to you, we would appreciate to have answer on the
utility of the informations we send you. If the administration has
the informations from other sources: OK! For the better.
But if they are of value, then you know, this kind of intelligence
informations involves costs that I am not anymore able to take
care of it and we have to decide jointly what to do.
It is exactly 2 years we met for the first time in Paris.
Inspite of the problems, we have enjoyed our conversation.

                                        Best regards,

~3~

1) With regard to the developments in the Middle East,
3 (three) meetings between Bin Laden, Al Zawaheri
and close advisors of the office of Khamnei have taken place in
Tehran. Those who have knowledge of the meetings are (a Rafsanjani
b) Nategh Nouri, c) a former, very high level of the Ministry of
intelligence, d) a selected groups of security forces (Rangers.)
The main issue of discussion has been how to counter the United
States, as they believe there will be a crisis with the
United States. The central decision reached <u>was to have
a terroristic action within the ~~United~~ United States.</u>
(Reference are previous fax, "dirty bombs."

2) A terrorist team has been sent to London to kill M͏r Fouladin
who runs a television against the regime in Tehran.
Project: By RPG or a car with explosives. No limits on
financial requirements for this project.

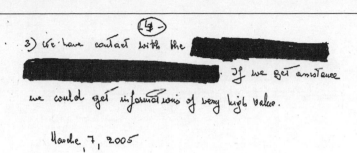

3) We have contact with the ████████████ ████████████ . If we get assistance we could get informations of very high value.

March, 7, 2005

(4)

3) We have contact with the ███████████████

███████████████████. If we get assistance

we could get informations of very high value.

March 7, 2005

⑤

Our source close to the coordination committee of Al-Qaeda - Iran informs us that ▮▮▮▮▮▮▮▮▮▮▮▮ within the USA, all important targets are being protected. Consequently two dirty bombs shall be used before the end of 2006; one within the US, one in the Persian Gulf close to Saudi Arabia. Transport of the bombs is no problem, they have a technical problem to solve which is related to the explosion of the bombe.

② Khamnei has issued orders that the distinction of the statue of freedom in New York is of top priority. ③ Khamnei has forbidden any talk and negociation concerning a deal Mojahedin against Bin Laden. ④ Bin Laden has been moved from North of Tehran, Damavand Area, (Ab-Sard, 10 km to the South of the city of Damavand) to another place. There are 3 iranian guards allways with him; they have instruction to kill him should the americans try to get hold on him, because in this case he could divulge Irans involvement.

⑤ At the US desk of the Foreign Ministry several american and an indian are cooperating with the Ministry. One of the american has travelled several times abroad. The last time he had a meeting in Kish island and received an important amount of money. the next meeting is projected abroad. ⑥ 3 people, in Paris, ▮▮▮▮▮▮▮▮▮▮▮▮▮▮▮▮▮▮▮▮▮▮ have purchased equipments for Irans atom program and sent them to Iran, they have been congratulated by Khamnei.

⑦ Several African doctors are cooperating with Tehran on terroristic activities. ⑧ Hotel Homa I (one) in Mashed has been declared closed on the pretext of reparation work. The reason is that the hotel has been taken over by ministry of intelligence: Al Qaeda members and other terrorists from Afghanistan stay there.

⑨ A video statement by Bin Laden will be shown soon. ⑩ In Irans security council, it has been decided that after presidential election opposition figures abroad will be killed. ――

Annex:
(6)

- (a) Plans have been prepared to hijack a plane
from Europe to USA (Germany, France or Britain.)

(b) Plans have been prepared to attack american ships.

March 7, 2005

Appendix Two

Memo: Ali a Credible Source

September 22, 2003

MEMO

TO: HASC Vice Chairman Curt Weldon

SUBJECT: "Ali" A Credible Source

"Ali" is the pseudonym of a foreign national who claims access to sensitive, inside information derived from high-ranking sources within the government of Iran. Ali claims access to information on Iran's programs for weapons of mass destruction and information on the plans of Iranian-sponsored terrorists. Iranian leadership views and international terrorism are among the toughest intelligence challenges facing the United States today. **Since Iran is the world's chief sponsor of international terrorists, and as the United States is presently engaged in a war on terrorism, any source with credible information could make a significant contribution to the national security of the United States.**

Some experts have challenged "Ali's" credibility and dismissed his allegations, claiming that "Ali's" predictions, that have generally proven correct, about Iranian and terrorist behavior are probably derived from press reports, and not from high-ranking informants within Teheran. However, a survey of press reports shows that "Ali's" predictions preceded the press reports and must have been derived from some other source not available to the world press.

The Congressional Research Service was tasked to conduct a thorough LEXIS-NEXIS search of all TV, radio, newspaper and other media worldwide to find their earliest reports on several major events that were successfully predicted by "Ali." The date of the earliest press reports were compared to the date of "Ali's" prediction of the event. "Ali" has consistently anticipated—before the world press—major developments in Iran's program for weapons of mass destruction and in threats from international terrorists. "Ali" has beaten the world press to headline stories on Iranian weapons of mass destruction and the terrorist threat often by a margin of weeks or months.

"Ali's" record of forecasting is consistent with his claim that he has access to sensitive, inside information derived from high-ranking sources within the government of Iran:

- On April 25, 2003, "Ali" alleged that Iran is negotiating to buy an atomic bomb from North Korea. One day later, on April 26, 2003, the world press first reported North Korea's announcement that it might sell atomic weapons.

- On April 25, 2003, "Ali" alleged that Iran was greatly accelerating its atomic bomb program. **Thirteen days later,** on May 8, 2003, the world press first reported that Iran had initiated a crash program to build an atomic bomb, including revised estimates to that effect by the U.S. Intelligence Community.

- On April 25, 2003, "Ali" alleged that Iranian delegations had recently visited North Korea several times to negotiate the purchase of an atomic bomb. **Forty-four days later**, on June 11, 2003, the world press first reported testimony from a North Korean defector that Iranians had recently visited North Korea several times to explore nuclear cooperation, including possibly the purchase of a North Korean A-bomb.

- On May 4, 2003, "Ali" alleged an imminent terrorist threat to the United States. **Sixteen days later**, on May 20, 2003, the world press first reported that U.S. homeland security was elevated to Orange Alert, based partly on intercepted communications indicating an imminent terrorist threat to the United States.

- On May 17, 2003, "Ali" alleged the existence of a terrorist plot to hijack an airplane in Canada to use in a suicide attack against a nuclear reactor in the United States. **Ninety-seven days later**, on August 22, 2003, the world press first reported the arrest in Canada of a terrorist cell engaged in pilot training, apparently for the purpose of a crashing an airplane into a nuclear reactor.

Letter of April 28, 2003

Sent to:

GEORGE TENET*
Director, Central Intelligence Agency

SPEAKER DENNIS J. HASTERT
Speaker, U.S. House Of Representatives

REP. PORTER GOSS
Chairman, House Permanent Select Committee on Intelligence

VICE ADMIRAL LOWELL E. JACOBY
Director, Defense Intelligence Agency

LT. GENERAL MICHAEL V. HAYDEN
Director, National Security Agency

*Since these letters are identical, only the letter to Tenet is shown.

CURT WELDON
7TH DISTRICT, PENNSYLVANIA

2466 RAYBURN HOUSE OFFICE BUILDING
WASHINGTON, DC 20515–3807
(202) 225-2011

1554 GARRETT ROAD
UPPER DARBY, PA 19082
(610) 259-0700

E-mail: curtpa07@mail.house.gov
www.house.gov/curtweldon

MIGRATORY BIRD
CONSERVATION COMMISSION
REPUBLICAN POLICY COMMITTEE

Congress of the United States
House of Representatives
Washington, DC 20515–3807

COMMITTEE ON ARMED SERVICES
MILITARY PROCUREMENT, CHAIRMAN
MILITARY READINESS
SPECIAL OVERSIGHT PANEL ON MERCHANT MARINE
SPECIAL OVERSIGHT PANEL ON TERRORISM

COMMITTEE ON SCIENCE
RESEARCH
ENVIRONMENT, TECHNOLOGY AND STANDARDS

CO-CHAIRMAN
CONGRESSIONAL FIRE SERVICES CAUCUS
DUMA–CONGRESS STUDY GROUP
GLOBE OCEAN PROTECTION TASK FORCE
CONGRESSIONAL DIABETES CAUCUS

April 28, 2003

The Honorable George Tenet
Director
Central Intelligence Agency

Dear Mr. Tenet:

On April 25, 2003, I met in Paris, France with ████████████████ a former high ranking official in Iran under the Shah, who claims to be well connected to knowledgeable and high ranking sources in Iran's present government. ████████████ during our meeting made a number of allegations, supposedly originating from authoritative sources within the present government of Iran. These allegations, if true, are so threatening and so important to the national security of the United States that I am obliged to draw them to your immediate attention. According to ████████

- The government of Iran plans to assassinate former President George Bush;

- The government of Iran is giving refuge to Osama Bin Laden in a safe house located near Teheran, in the northern suburb of Pasdaran;

- Iran is pursuing a crash program to develop an atomic bomb, and hopes to be able to test an atomic weapon by September 2003;

- Iran is currently negotiating to buy an atomic bomb from North Korea;

- Iran has acquired a missile with a range in excess of 3,500 kilometers from North Korea; and

- The government of Iran plans to assassinate Yasser Arafat sometime within the next month.

I urge the CIA to interview ████████ and assess the credibility of his allegations. This assessment should be done by the CIA independently, not relying upon any foreign intelligence service, such as the French Ministry of Interior, that may have ulterior motives in assessing ████████ allegations.

There are reasons for questioning ███████████ credibility. ██████████ is offering to purchase intelligence from Iranian officials through bribery. ███

However, there are also weighty reasons for giving credence to ███████ claims. ████████ is a former member of Iran's political elite. ███████████████████████████████████████ For twenty years, since his exile from Iran, ████████████ appears to have been active among the Iranian ex-patriate community plotting the overthrow of the present Iranian government and cultivating intelligence sources within that government. ████████████ claim that Iran is negotiating to buy an A-bomb from North Korea preceded, and resonates disturbingly with, North Korea's recent assertion of its right to sell nuclear weapons to other countries.

Attached find a transcript of my meeting with ████████████ on April 25 and materials provided by ████████████ at that meeting.

Sincerely,

CURT WELDON
Member of Congress

Letter to CIA Director George Tenet
April 14, 2004

CURT WELDON
7TH DISTRICT, PENNSYLVANIA

2466 RAYBURN HOUSE OFFICE BUILDING
WASHINGTON, DC 20515–3807
(202) 225–2011

1554 GARRETT ROAD
UPPER DARBY, PA 19082
(610) 259–0700

83 WEST 4TH STREET
BRIDGEPORT, PA 19405
(610) 270–1486

E-mail: curtpa07@mail.house.gov
www.house.gov/curtweldon

MIGRATORY BIRD
CONSERVATION COMMISSION
REPUBLICAN POLICY COMMITTEE

Congress of the United States
House of Representatives
Washington, DC 20515–3807

COMMITTEE ON ARMED SERVICES
TACTICAL AIR AND LAND FORCES, CHAIRMAN
STRATEGIC FORCES

COMMITTEE ON SCIENCE
SPACE AND AERONAUTICS
ENERGY

SELECT COMMITTEE ON
HOMELAND SECURITY

CO-CHAIRMAN:
CONGRESSIONAL FIRE SERVICES CAUCUS
DUMA – CONGRESS STUDY GROUP
GLOBE OCEAN PROTECTION TASK FORCE
CONGRESSIONAL DIABETES CAUCUS
HOMELAND SECURITY CAUCUS

April 14, 2004

The Honorable George Tenet
Director of Central Intelligence
Central Intelligence Agency
Washington, D.C. 20505

Dear Director Tenet:

Attached find the latest communication from ███████████, a former high official in Iran under the Shah, warning of developing threats to the United States in Iraq, and of a possible new threat to the U.S. homeland. ███████ claims to have at least two highly placed sources in the present Iranian government with access to the most sensitive information on Iran's support of international terrorism and programs for developing weapons of mass destruction. According to ███████ letter of April 12, 2004:

- Iran currently is supporting an Al Qaeda cell in the United States that is ready to execute a major terrorist attack on receiving orders from Teheran. Iran's leaders think that the 9-11 Commission hearings have so undermined political support for President Bush in the war on terrorism that another terrorist attack on the U.S. homeland might be enough to ensure the President's defeat in the next election—a key foreign policy objective of the government of Iran.

- Iran is supporting the violence in Iraq against the United States, with the objective of forcing the United States into a humiliating retreat, as in Somalia. The government of Iran has recently paid $70 million to bankroll al-Sadr's militia.

- The rash of hostage takings currently underway in Iraq was planned in Iran, supported by Iran's establishment of 56 "centers of intelligence and action" in Iraq, and coordinated with "experts for hostage taking" from Lebanon's Hezbollah that are now in Iraq.

- Iran owns one or more journalists working for the Arabic television network "Al-Jazeera" and has recently paid $18 million to finance an anti-American media campaign.

THIS STATIONERY PRINTED ON PAPER MADE OF RECYCLED FIBERS

I share the above information in the interests of exercising due diligence and providing warning of an imminent threat to U.S. interests abroad and at home.

As you know—or should know—I have been receiving information from this source for over a year. In April 2003, after I first met ███████ I immediately contacted your and other agencies to alert them that ██████ appeared to be a valuable resource in the war on terrorism. In November 2003, I provided to the House and Senate intelligence committees a record of ███████ reports and an analysis of their accuracy. Although some of ██ allegations have not materialized, his predictions of Iranian government behavior and terrorist plots have proven accurate most of the time. To cite just one example, on May 17, 2003, ██████ alleged the existence of a terrorist plot to hijack an airliner in Canada to use in a suicide attack against a nuclear reactor in the United States. Three months later, in August 2003, a terrorist cell was arrested in Canada that was engaged in pilot training, apparently for the purpose of crashing an airplane into a nuclear reactor.

██████ record of forecasting is consistent with his claim that he has access to sensitive, inside information derived from high-ranking sources within the government of Iran. Yet ██████ reward for seeking to help the U.S. government in the war on terrorism has been to be chastised by a CIA officer for talking to a member of Congress and to be chastised by the French Ministry of Interior for the same misdemeanor.

Frankly, I do not understand why CIA has not yet established, and appears determined never to establish, a working relationship with ██████. Surely, in the war on terrorism, we need all the help that we can get.

Sincerely,

CURT WELDON
Member of Congress

Appendix Five

Letter to John Hamre
Deputy Secretary of Defense
on National Operations Analysis Hub (NOAH)
July 30, 1999

‹L. • 7^r•DI•TRICT||(PEHNISYL VAPHA

2682 Rayburn House Office Building
Washington, DC 20515-3807
(202) 225-2011

1884 Garrett Road
Upper Darby, PA 19082
(610) 259-0700

30 South Valley Road, Suite 213
Paoli, PA 19301
(610) 640-9064

MIGRATORY BIRD
CONSERVATION COMMISSION
REPUBLICAN POLICY COMMITTEE
E-mail curt.pa7@hr.house.gov

Congress of the United States
House of Representatives
Washington, DC 20515–3807

COMMITTEE ON NATIONAL SECURITY
RESEARCH AND DEVELOPMENT, CHAIRMAN
READINESS
MERCHANT MARINE PANEL

COMMITTEE ON SCIENCE
ENERGY AND ENVIRONMENT
BASIC RESEARCH

CO-CHAIRMAN:
CONGRESSIONAL FIRE SERVICES CAUCUS
US-FSU ENERGY CAUCUS
THE EMPOWERMENT CAUCUS
GLOBE OCEAN PROTECTION TASK FORCE
CONGRESSIONAL MISSILE DEFENSE CAUCUS

July 30, 1999

The Honorable John Hamre
Deputy Secretary of Defense
Room 3E944
The Pentagon
Washington, D.C. 20301-1010

Dear Dr. Hamre:

I believe the time has come to create a central national level entity that can acquire, fuse and anaylze disparate data from many agencies in order to support the policymaker in taking action against threats from terrorism, proliferation, illegal technology diversions, espionage, narcotics, information warfare and cyberterrorism. These challenges are beginning to overlap, thereby blurring their distinction while posing increasing threats to our Nation.

Before we take action to counter these emerging threats, we must first understand their relationship to one another, their patterns, the people and countries involved, and the level of danger posed to our Nation. The Department of Defense has a unique opporuntiy to create a centralized national center that can do this for the country. It would be patterned after the Army's Land InformationWarfare Activity (LIWA) at Fort Belvoir, but would operate on a much broader scale. This entity would allow for near-time information and analysis to flow to a central fusion center, which I would designate the National Operations Analysis Hub (NOAH). I think this title it fitting, as NOAH will be provide a central hub built to protect our nation from the flood of threats.

NOAH would be comprised of a system of agency-specified mini-centers, or "pods" of participating agencies and services associated with growing national security concerns (attachment 1). NOAH would link the policymaker with action recommendations derived from fused information provided by the individual pods. NOAH would provide the automation and connectivity to allow the pods to talk together, share data and perspectives on a given situation in a near real-time, computer-based environment.

Along with its system of connected agency pod sites, NOAH would permit the display of collaborative threat profiling and analytical assessments on a large screen. It would be a national level operations and control center with a mission to intergrate various imagery, data and analytical viewpoints for decision-makers in support of national actions. I see NOAH as going beyond the capability of the National Military Command Center (NMCC) and the National Joint Military Intelligence Command (NJMIC), providing recommended courses of action that allow us to effectively meet those emerging challenges from asymmetrical threats in near real-time. Given its mission, I believe that NOAH should reside in the Office of the Secretary of Defense (Attachment 2).

I am aware of the initiative to link counterintelligence groups throughout the community. I am also aware of the counterterrorism center at the CIA, the new National Infrastructure Protection Center at the FBI, and a new HUMINT special operations center. I have heard of an attempt to connect the Office of Drug Control Policy (ONDCP) and OSD assets with federal, state and local law enforcement agencies. I also have seen what the Army has done at LIWA, which has created a foundation for creating a higher-level architecture collaborating all of these efforts. Each of these independent efforts needs to be coordinated at the national level. I believe LIWA has created a model that should be used as a basis for creating the participating agency pod sites.

I do not expect that establishment of NOAH should exceed $10 million. Each agency involved could set up its own pod to connect with the central NOAH site or to exchange data with any of its participants. Each agency could dedicate monies to establish their own pod site, while the $50 million available in DARPA for related work could be used to establish the NOAH structure immediately.

The NOAH concept of a national collaborative environment supporting policy and decision-makers mirrors the ideas you have expressed to me in recent discussions, and it is a tangible way to confront the growing assymetrical threats to our nation. I have a number of ideas regarding staffing options and industry collaboration, and would appreciate the opportunity to discuss them with you. Thank you for your consideration. I look forward to hearing from you at your earliest convenience.

Sincerely,

CURT WELDON
Member of Congress

The NOAH center in the Office of the Secretary of Defense would be comprised of representatives from an initial cluster of pod sites to include: CIA, DIA, National Imagery and Mapping Agency (NIMA), NSA, NRO, Defense Threat Reduction Agency (DTSA), JCS, Army, Air Force, Navy, Marine Corps, ONDCP, FBI, DEA, Customs, National Criminal Investigative Service (NCIS), National Infrastructure Protection Center, Defense Information Systems Agency (DISA), State, the five CINCS, DOE, INS, Commerce, Treasury.

Elements which would be connected into NOAH would include the White House Situation Room, a Congressional Virtual Hearing Room and a possible redundant (back up) site.

The benefits of creating a NOAH include:

a. For national policy makers, a national collaborative environment offers situations updates across a variety of issues and offers suggested courses of action, based on analysis, to help government officials make more informed decisions.

b. For the Intelligence Community, a national collaborative environment will help end stovepiping and create more robust strategic analyses as well as near real-time support to field operations.

c. For military commanders and planners, a national collaborative environment offers full battlefield visualization, threat profiling, robust situational awareness, as well as near real-timer support to special missions such as peacekeeping, humanitarian aid, national emergencies or special operations.

d. For law enforcement, a national collaborative environment provides investigative and threat profiling support, and field station situational awareness.

Appendix Six

U.S.–Russia Partnership

U.S.-RUSSIA PARTNERSHIP
A New Time
A New Beginning

Summary of Recommendations

AGRICULTURAL DEVELOPMENT

- Assist in agricultural production.
- Expand private-sector investment.
- Enhance capacity to purchase essential agricultural inputs, commodities and equipment.

CULTURAL/EDUCATIONAL DEVELOPMENT

- Expand cultural ties outside the major cities.
- Assist regional museums in generating tourism.
- Provide for more Russian language and cultural studies in U.S. schools.

DEFENSE AND SECURITY

- Initiate new bilateral talks similar to the Ross-Mamedov talks on a Global Protection System.
- Move forward with joint talks on a new nonproliferation regime.
- Encourage progress on the RAMOS program and restructure the Nuclear Cities Initiative.

ECONOMIC DEVELOPMENT

- Help facilitate Russia's accession to the WTO and its acceptance of all WTO agreements.
- Increase funding for OPIC and EX-IM Bank projects in Russia.
- Work with Russia to improve intellectual property rights.

4   U.S.-RUSSIA PARTNERSHIP — *A New Time, A New Beginning*

Therefore, in consultation with many of the leading experts on Russia, I propose a series of initiatives to engage Russia on issues like the environment, energy, economic development, and health care — as well as defense and security. Some of these are new ideas, but many are not. Many of these initiatives are already underway, and need additional support to make even greater progress.

■

Such engagement is in the interest of the U.S. as well as Russia. For if the U.S. and Russia are cooperating on issues across the board, Russia will be more likely to work closely with America on the national security issues that matter most to us — missile defense, the war against terrorism, and proliferation.

■

This is not, and will never be, a finished product. The contours of our bilateral relationship change daily with world events. Nor will it likely be turned into a grand legislative proposal, although certainly parts of it may be. I hope only that it is a starting point for discussions between Russia and America on ways that we can forge a new relationship that will benefit both our countries.

■

For if we make a new American-Russian relationship, one based on common interests that benefit the citizens of both countries, then we will make great progress — not just for America and Russia alone, but for peace and stability across the globe.

Rep. Curt Weldon (R-PA)

INTRODUCTION

A New Vision for U.S.-Russian Relations

Those of us who value the U.S.-Russian relationship have been on a roller-coaster ride for the past decade. During the heady days of the fall of the Berlin Wall and the ensuing collapse of the Soviet Union, it appeared that our two countries would cooperate as never before. The world cheered when Presidents Bush and Yeltsin hailed a new "strategic partnership" between America and Russia.

∎

There followed, however, a dark period — marked by misguided American policies and rampant Russian corruption. The Russian economy sagged as American aid — money meant for the Russian people — was siphoned off and stashed in Swiss banks and American real estate investment. At the same time, NATO's war in Kosovo strained the already sinking bilateral relationship. What were the results of this increasingly bitter disenchantment? A more aggressive Russian foreign policy, increased proliferation from Moscow to rogue states, and the final *coup de grace:* Russia and China announcing last year a new "strategic partnership" — against the interests of America and the West.

∎

Now is the time, with new leaders in Washington and Moscow, to improve the relationship for the long-term.

My interest in this relationship began when I was nineteen years old, when a college professor convinced me to switch my major to Russian Studies. Since that time, I have been fascinated with the Soviet Union and Russia — and have traveled there more than twenty-five times.

■

I began my travels when I was a member of my local County Council and was invited to travel to Moscow by the American Council of Young Political Leaders. I have continued to visit Russia since my election to Congress, as a member of the House Armed Services Committee, and later as co-chairman of the Duma-Congress Study Group, the official interparliamentary exchange between the U.S. and Russia.

■

My interactions with leaders across Russia have taught me that the Russians are a proud people, historically aware, and mindful of Russia's unique global role. Increasingly, they are becoming aware of the limitless possibilities for U.S.-Russian cooperation on a host of issues.

■

This brief paper, then, is an effort to weave together a comprehensive program of U.S.-Russian cooperation across a wide-range of issues.

■

Too often, the focus of our bilateral relations has been on defense and security — precisely the issues on which our interests often collide. It would be more useful, as we move forward with a Russian policy for the 21st century, to take a more holistic approach — one that takes into account Russia's myriad concerns as well as our own.

Congress of the United States
House of Representatives
Washington, DC 20515
November 7, 2001

President George W. Bush
1600 Pennsylvania Avenue, NW
Washington, DC 20500

Dear President Bush:

As you prepare for the upcoming summit with President Putin, we commend the positive approach you have established with Russia. Too often, the focus of our bilateral relations has been on defense and security – precisely the issues on which our interests often collide. It would be more useful, as we move forward with a Russian policy for the 21st century to take a more holistic approach – one that takes into account Russia's myriad concerns as well as our own.

Therefore, in consultation with many of the leading experts on Russia, we propose a series of bipartisan initiatives to engage Russia on issues such as the environment, energy, economic development, health care – as well as defense and security. We call this proposal "A New Time, A New Beginning." Some of these are new ideas, but many are not. Many of these initiatives are already underway, and need additional support to make even greater progress.

Such engagement is in the U.S. interest as well as Russia's. If the United States and Russia cooperate on issues across the board, Russia will be more likely to work closely with America on the national security issues that matter most to us – missile defense, the war against terrorism, and proliferation.

We encourage you to review the enclosed proposal and hope that some of these initiatives will prove useful to you in the ongoing discussions between Russia and America. We look forward to working with you to forge a new relationship that will benefit both our countries.

Thank you for your consideration of this request.

Sincerely,

PRINTED ON RECYCLED PAPER

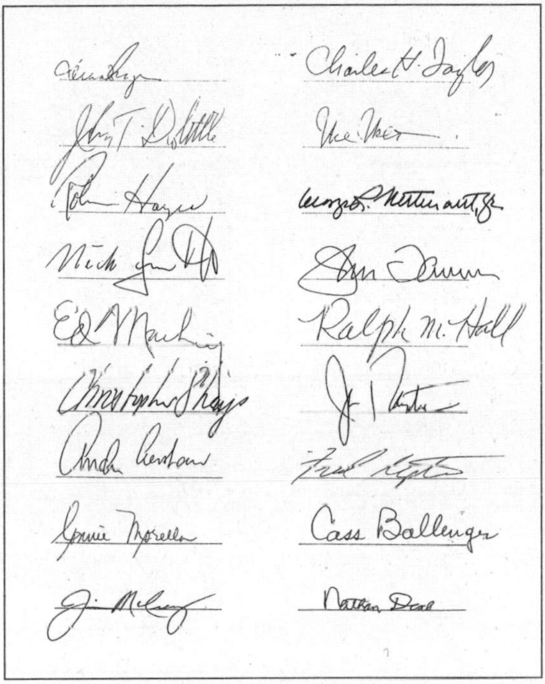
Ralph M. Hall
Cass Ballenger

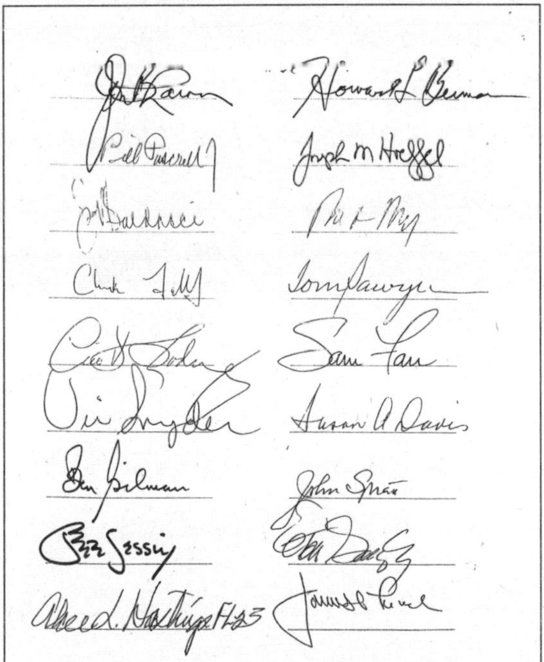
Howard L. Berman
Susan A. Davis

Page 1:
Sen Biden   Curt Weldon
Sen Lugar   Sen Levin

Page 2:
Silvestre Reyes   Joe Pitts
Cliff Stearns   Todd Platts
Mike Pence   John Murtha
Tim Holden   Bob Schaffer
Dick Armey   Dave Hobson
Dennis Kucinich   Brian Kerns
Felix Grucci   Ellen Tauscher
Roscoe Bartlett   Neil Abercrombie
James Hansen   Don Sherwood

Page 3:
Maurice Hinchey   Dana Rohrabacher
Mike Castle   Bud Cramer
Mac Thornberry   Chris Cox
Corrine Brown   Chet Edwards
Bob Clement   Solomon Ortiz
JC Watts   John Peterson
Marcy Kaptur   Henry Hyde
John Linder   Roger Wicker
Walter Jones   Mark Souder

Page 4:
John Larson   Howard Berman
Bill Pascrell   Joseph Hoeffel
John Baldacci   Bob Ney
Chaka Fattah   Tom Sawyer
Ciro Rodriguez   Sam Farr
Vic Snyder   Susan Davis
Ben Gilman   John Spratt
Pete Sessions   Elton Gallegly
Alcee Hastings   James Leach

Page 5:
Deborah Pryce   Charles Taylor
John Dolittle   Ike Skelton
Robin Hayes   George Nethercutt Jr
Nick Smith   John Tanner
Edward Markey   Ralph Hall
Christopher Shays   Jim Ramstad
Ander Crenshaw   Fred Upton

Connie Morella   Cass Ballenger
Jim Maloney   Nathan Deal

Page 6:
Jerry Weller   Tom Davis
Jim Gibbons   Randy Cunningham
Jim Ryun   Gary Condit
Judy Biggert   Randy Forbes
Jerry Costello   Steven LaTourette
Eddie Bernice Johnson   Joe Skeen
Stepehn Horn   Bob Borski
Kay Granger   Lincoln Diaz-Balart
Ed Scrock   Chris Smith

Page 7:
Adam Putnam   Jim Saxton
Frank Pallone   Jim Turner
Ed Schrock   Mike Ferguson
Johnny Isakson   Van Hilleary
Robert Andrews   Ed Royce
Bernie Sanders   Bob Filner
Nick Lampson   Luis Gutierrez
Rod Blagojevich   Danny Davis

Page 8:
Jane Harman   Hilda Solis
Rick Boucher   Rush Holt
Christopher John   Carrie Meek
Todd Akin   Amo Houghton
Dave Weldon   Paul Kanjorski
Bart Gordon   Bob Goodlatte
Virgil Goode Jr   Doug Bereuter
Alan Mollohan   John Shimkus
Frank Wolf   J.D. Hayworth

Page 9:
James Greenwood   Tom Allen
Kevin Brady   George Gekas
Bob Brady   Robert Andrews
Melissa Hart   Mike Doyle
Phil English   Shelly Moore Capito
John Thune   Rob Simmons
                                Todd Akin

INDEX

Emirates. *See* United Arab Emirates
EMP. *See* electromagnetic pulse
attack
EMP Commission. *See* Commission to Assess the Threat to the
United States from Electromagnetic Pulse (EMP) Attack
Energy Department, U.S., 164,
169, 189
Eslami, 37
Etellaat Elami, 36
Europe, 46; Iran relations with,
34; Islam in, 130; terrorist plans
for attacks in, 5

F
Fallahian, Ayatollah, 36, 80
Fallujah, Iraq, 72
FBI. *See* Federal Bureau of Inves-
tigation
Federal Bureau of Investigation
(FBI), 8, 153; Ali and, 158;
Global Relief Organization and,
68; intelligence reform and, 17;
Kosovo war and, 16–17; plot to
assassinate Bush, George H. W.
and, 73; potential intelligence
sources and, 3. *See also* intelli-
gence community
15 Khordad, 39
First Gulf War, 13
Foreign Broadcast Information
Service, 10
*Foreign Missile Threats: Analytic
Soundness of Certain National
Intelligence Estimates*, 161–62

France: French Ministry of Interior, 8, 50, 73–76; Iran and, 75,
83; Iran WMD program and, 97
freedom: Iran and, 33; war on
terrorism and, 196–200
French Ministry of Interior, 8, 50,
73–76

G
GAO. *See* General Accounting
Office
General Accounting Office
(GAO), 161–62
Germany, 74, 97, 125, 130, 137,
145, 146
Ghom, Iran, 32, 40, 60–61, 74,
76, 79, 98, 104, 123
Global Relief Organization, 68
Golestan, Iran, 27
Golpaygani, Ayatollah, 36
Gorbanifar, Manucher, 4, 12
Goss, Porter, 8, 11, 117, 151–52,
182
Guardian of Revolution, 92, 136,
148, 149
Guardians of the Revolution, 29,
40, 71, 79

H
Haiti, 169
Hakim, Mohammed Bagher Al,
60
Hakim, Muhssen, 60, 136
Hakmatyar, Mullah Omar, 95
Hamas: Committee of Nine and,
29, 31; terrorist super-organiza-
tion and, 54, 60, 78

terrorism (continued):
  Iran and, 13, 34, 60; martyrdom and, 25, 111; nuclear reactors and, 63–70; prevention of,
  2; radiation poisoning and,
  9–10, 49, 63–70; Russia and,
  193–94; Seabrook Nuclear
  Reactor plot, 9–10, 63–70, 82,
  91, 93, 96; suicide, 25; technology and, 157; training camps
  for, 81; WMD and, 157,
  160–61. *See also* war on
  terrorism
Terrorist Threat Integration Center (TTIC), 19
Thailand, 48
Tikrit, Barzan Ibrahim al, 21
Toronto, Canada, 9
Toronto 19, 67–70
Treasury Department, U.S., 88
Trulock, Notra, 169–70
TTIC. *See* Terrorist Threat Integration Center
Tunisia, 81
Turkey, 40, 48, 61, 116, 136
Turkmenistan, 61
12th Imam plot, 2, 14, 98, 149;
  2004 U.S. presidential election
  and, 103; al Qaeda and,
  109–10; Bush, George W. and,
  110; code name for, 103; Committee of Nine and, 94–95, 97,
  103, 110, 113–15; drugs and,
  110; intelligence on, 3, 158;
  Khameni, Ayatollah and, 99,
  110, 113–15; postponement of,
  91, 113–15

U

UAE. *See* United Arab Emirates
Ukraine, Chernobyl incident in,
  9–10, 49, 65–67
UN. *See* United Nations
United Arab Emirates (UAE), 48
United Nations (UN), 47, 66,
  101; Global Relief Organization
  and, 68; International Atomic
  Energy Agency of, 104, 109,
  115, 128; Iran WMD program
  and, 125, 197
United States: 2004 presidential
  election in, 91, 98, 103, 114; al
  Qaeda in, 27, 122, 131, 133,
  134; Iran, war with, and,
  12–13, 22, 196–98; Iran relations with, 34, 48–49, 59, 80,
  99, 101, 118, 122, 143; Iran
  strategy against, 24–27, 29–31;
  Russian alliance with, 192–95;
  terrorist plots against, 1, 2, 5,
  14–15, 91, 94–95
UN Security Council, 115
U.S. News and World Report, 6
Uzbekistan, 40

V

Velayati, 36, 39, 71, 80, 107
Vienna, Austria, 15–16

W

war on terrorism: in Afghanistan,
  12; Canada and, 68–69;
  exploitation of, 3; freedom and,
  196–200; intelligence community and, 153, 190–92; in Iraq,